T5-CCU-744

She was drowning . . .

With no one on the remote beach to help her, Chelsea knew she was doomed. Slipping again under the sea, she held her breath until her lungs felt on fire. *I can't. hold out any longer. It's all over. I'm going to die.*

But then, out of nowhere, she was yanked by the top of her T-shirt and pulled to the surface. Gagging, sputtering, and coughing, Chelsea gulped life-giving air into her burning lungs. *Oh, thank goodness, someone has saved me!* Totally exhausted and too weak to utter anything but, "Don't let go of me," Chelsea turned around to see who had rescued her — and couldn't believe her eyes.

It wasn't a person — it was a dog!

HAUNTED ANIMALS

TRUE GHOST STORIES

by ALLAN ZULLO

SCHOLASTIC INC.

New York   Toronto   London   Auckland   Sydney
Mexico City   New Delhi   Hong Kong   Buenos Aires

To Maggie Spicer, a hauntingly sweet little girl.
— Allan Zullo

No part of this publication may be reproduced, stored in a retrieval system, or transmitted in any form or by any means, electronic, mechanical, photocopying, recording, or otherwise, without written permission of the publisher. For information regarding permission, write to Scholastic Inc., Attention: Permissions Department, 557 Broadway, New York, NY 10012.

ISBN 0-439-68058-1

Copyright © 1995 by Nash and Zullo Productions, Inc. All rights reserved. Published by Scholastic Inc. SCHOLASTIC and associated logos are trademarks and/or registered trademarks of Scholastic Inc.

12 11 10 9 8 7 6 5 4 3 2 1   5 6 7 8 9 10/0

Printed in the U.S.A.   40

First Scholastic printing, February 2005

Cover illustrations by Patrick Faricy
Cover design by Jennifer Rinaldi Windau

CONTENTS

Could Animals Be Ghosts?

Some kids claim they have seen ghosts. In most cases, according to investigators, these hauntings involve the spirit of a dead person. But every once in a while, a kid reports that the ghost he or she saw was different—because the phantom was an *animal*!

Haunted Animals is a spooky collection of stories about kids who claim to have encountered spirits from the animal world— including pet dogs, a loving cat, a wild horse, and a vengeful wolf. You'll read nine spine-tingling tales, inspired, in part, by the accounts of those who say they were haunted. The names and places in the stories have been changed to protect everyone's privacy.

Could animals really be ghosts? You might think so after reading the eerie stories in this book!

TWISTER'S FAREWELL

" Twister! Get your loop-de-loop! It's time to swing!"

Thirteen-year-old Tracy Chandler had opened the back door and yelled out to her fun-loving brown and white fox terrier, who was busy sniffing at a freshly dug gopher hole. The dog's ears stood up when he heard his owner's voice. With a happy yelp, he scampered up the back porch. He made a quick search of the area and then let out another bark when he found his favorite toy—a sturdy two-foot-long (.6 m) rope with a loop on each end.

Then, with his head held high, he pranced to the back-yard to begin his daily ritual with Tracy—a quick game of tug-of-war. Tracy, barefoot and wearing a California Angels T-shirt over her blue cut-offs, stuffed her long hair under a baseball cap. Then she got down on her knees and grabbed one loop of the rope while Twister locked his jaws on the other end.

"Are you ready, Twister?" she asked. The dog responded with a playful "grrrrr." And the game was on. With his hind legs pushing back, Twister shook his head and tried to pull his owner across the lawn. Tracy let him think he was winning before she began yanking him toward her. Finally, after a few minutes of tug-of-war, Tracy rose to her feet while still holding onto the rope. It was time for the big finale.

Twister was not about to let go, even though he was now standing on his hind legs. He kept growling and shaking the rope. Using both hands, Tracy held the rope up higher and higher until the dog was completely off the ground. But Twister's jaws remained firmly clamped on the loop.

"Okay, Twister, hang on. Let's go for a spin!"

Tracy then began twirling while holding onto the rope. With his ears flying, the dog whirled around several times. In the four years that Twister had been Tracy's pet, never once had he let go. When Tracy began feeling dizzy, she slowed her twirl and gently let Twister return to the ground. But the dog refused to give up the rope. He would wait her out. Like always, Tracy had to give in first. "You win, Twister."

Only when he heard those words did he let go of the rope. Then he barked in triumph and wagged his tail. He picked up the rope and returned it to the porch.

"Tracy!" her mother called out from the kitchen door. "Tommy is on the phone."

"Tommy?" she said. "I'll be right there!" Tommy was the new kid in school, and Tracy had a crush on him.

"Be back in a minute, Twister," Tracy told her dog. A half hour later, she returned to Twister, carrying her in-line skates. She sat on the back step, slipped on knee pads and elbow pads, and then laced up the skates. "Hey, Twister, I'm going *skating*"—she put extra emphasis on the word—"over to the park to meet Tommy. Want to come along with me?"

Normally, whenever he heard the word "skating," Twister would hop around, bark, and wag his tail. He loved to run beside Tracy when she skated up and down the street.

But today, Twister stared at her and whined loudly, almost frantically. Tracy had seen that pleading look in her dog's eyes and heard that heart-wrenching whine only one other time. It happened four years ago on the worst day, up to then, in Tracy's and Twister's lives.

* * *

Back then Twister was a puppy, and he had a different name: Baxter. He had been part of the Chandler family for only a few weeks.

Before going off to school on that fateful day, Tracy had fed him and played with him in the fenced-in backyard. He was as frisky as usual, but when it was time for Tracy to go, the dog began whining, barking, and trying to jump on her.

"Baxter, I've got to go to school now," Tracy said. "I'll be back this afternoon, and we can play some more."

The dog continued to whine. Not in a begging way for more attention, but more like a fearful whimper. "Is something wrong, Baxter? Are you hurting?" Tracy examined his coat and felt his bones, but he didn't appear to be in any physical discomfort. Nevertheless, Tracy could tell that her dog was troubled.

She went inside and returned with a doggie bone. "Here's an extra treat. Now be a good boy, and I'll see you in a few hours. I'll run straight home from school as fast as I can, so we can play some more."

As she closed the gate behind her, Tracy had an uneasy feeling that something bad was going to happen to her sweet puppy. She walked around to the front of the house where her parents were getting into their cars to go to work. "Mom, Dad, is there any way we can leave Baxter inside the house?"

"Why, honey?"

"I don't know. He seems scared of something, and I've just got this feeling that he might get hurt or . . ."

"He'll be just fine. He loves it outside. If it rains, he can always stay dry on the porch. We can't leave him alone inside. He's still a puppy. Besides, he loves being outside. Want a ride to school?"

"No, thanks."

Before walking the three blocks to school, Tracy quietly went behind the house and peeked through a slat in the fence to check on her dog. He seemed okay as he aimlessly sniffed around a bush.

Throughout the day, Tracy couldn't help but feel uneasy. Her mind seemed totally focused on her little dog, fretting that something terrible would happen. Around 2 P.M., she had reason to worry. A fierce thunderstorm blew in, battering the area with heavy rain and lightning.

"May I have your attention please," said the school principal, Mrs. Marley, over the classroom loudspeakers. "Students and teachers, we have just been informed by the police that a tornado has touched down a few miles from here. Please leave your classrooms immediately and in an orderly fashion just as we've practiced in our drills. Go into the hallway and sit quietly on the floor."

As the kids in her class scrambled away from their desks, Tracy's mind jangled with fear—for herself, her classmates, and most of all . . .

"Baxter!" Tracy shouted out loud. "Oh my gosh! He's all alone at home. I've got to go get him!" She rushed out of the classroom and headed for the front door, but Mrs. Marley stopped her. "Tracy, you know the drill. Get back into the hallway."

"But, Mrs. Marley, my dog, he's in the backyard and—"

"Tracy, you can't leave now. It's storming outside, and we're under a tornado warning."

"But—"

Just then they heard an enormous roar similar to a freight train barrelling down the tracks. "It's a twister!" shouted Mrs. Marley. She grabbed Tracy and dashed into the hallway. Within seconds, the doors rattled, the windows shattered, the school shook, and the younger kids screamed. And then it was suddenly over.

Fortunately, everyone in the school was safe because the howling tornado had missed the building by only 300 yards (273 m). When the shaken kids finally had a chance to peek through the broken windows, they were stunned by the destruction outside. The twister had uprooted trees, rolled over a half dozen cars, snapped power lines, and smashed into several homes.

Within minutes, Tracy's parents arrived at the school to make sure their daughter was all right. Then they all hurried over to their house. They had to go on foot because there was too much debris on the streets, making it unsafe to drive.

When they arrived home, they cried. The tornado had ripped open one side of their house and collapsed the roof. As shocked as she was by the damage, Tracy had a bigger fear on her mind.

"Baxter! Baxter! Where are you?" She raced around to the backyard, where the fence had been flattened and the porch demolished. Frantically, Tracy began lifting pieces of wood, siding, and roofing in a desperate search for her puppy. Her parents joined in, but no one could find the dog anywhere.

"He must be alive, honey," said her father, trying to comfort Tracy. "Maybe he took off running when the fence fell down."

"Daddy, Baxter knew something bad was going to happen. He tried to warn me this morning. I could tell. Oh, where is he? Where is he?"

Tracy ran down the street, stopping neighbors and asking them if they had seen her dog. They all shook their heads. When Tracy headed home, Mrs. Young, who lived behind the Chandlers, asked her, "What are you looking for?"

"My little dog, Baxter," Tracy replied.

"Is he a brown and white puppy?"

"Yes, have you seen him?"

Mrs. Young hesitated and turned her eyes away from Tracy. "Mrs. Young," Tracy repeated. "Have you seen him?"

Mrs. Young sighed and said, "When the tornado came through and hit your house, I saw a brown and white furry ball get sucked up. I didn't know what it was at first. The puppy was about 20 feet (6 m) up in the air when I realized it was a dog."

Tracy burst into tears, ran into the arms of her mother, and sobbed.

"Honey, I feel so badly for you," said her mom, trying to comfort her. "The poor thing."

"Mom, I know our house is wrecked, but right now my dog is the most important thing to me. I've got to find him." Tracy dragged her bicycle out of the damaged garage, hopped on, and began riding around the neighborhood, following the path of destruction left by the tornado. A half hour later, on a quiet street near the edge of town, Tracy screeched to a stop.

There, in front of her, was Baxter—wet, tired, and dazed, but otherwise not injured.

"Baxter! You're alive! You're alive!"

The puppy yelped joyously as Tracy leapt off her bike and scooped him up in her arms. Whining happily, Baxter covered her face in licks. "Oh, I'm so happy to see you!" Tracy cried with relief as she squeezed him tightly.

Two things changed for the dog following his scary ordeal. From that day on, he slept with Tracy on her bed. And he underwent a name change. "You're no longer Baxter," Tracy announced. "Starting right now, we're going to call you Twister!"

The terrier barked twice as if he totally agreed with his new name.

* * *

Now it was four years later. Tracy's heart sank when she looked into Twister's eyes and saw the same fear he had displayed on the day of the tornado. She tried to pretend it was her imagination. But she could tell by his behavior that he was worried.

Twister ran around in circles and then jumped on his mistress. "What are you trying to tell me? What's wrong?" she asked.

Tracy looked up at the sky. It was a beautiful summer day, not a cloud in the sky. *It can't be another tornado,* she told herself. *Something is bugging him, but what? Am I supposed to pass up the chance to skate with Tommy? What would I tell him? That my dog is acting crazy, so I have to stay home? No way.*

Tracy finished lacing her in-line skates and said, "Twister, I've got to go. Are you coming?"

The dog ran onto the porch and snatched his loop-de-loop and dropped it at her feet. Tracy kneeled down, gently held her dog's head in her hand, and said, "I can't play tug-of-war with you now, Twister. We finished that game. I'm going skating now."

As Tracy headed toward the sidewalk, Twister let out a high-pitched bark, almost like a warning. He started to run after her, stopped, and whined. Then he picked up his loop-de-loop and took off in a mad dash until he caught up with his mistress.

"So you decided to join me after all, huh?" said Tracy with a big grin. "Good, I'd like you to meet Tommy. He's a cool guy." Looking into her dog's eyes, she added, "Don't worry. You and I will be extra careful. Nothing is going to happen to us."

In her neighborhood, the sidewalk ended two blocks from her house, so Tracy had to skate in the street. She rolled along next to the curb and ordered Twister to run alongside her on the grass. When they reached Central Avenue—the busiest street between her home and the park—they waited at the stop light. When it turned green, she picked Twister up in her arms and started across.

They never made it to the other side.

A speeding car, operated by a drunk driver, failed to notice that the traffic signal had turned red until it was too late. Seeing the girl and her dog in his path, the driver honked his horn and slammed on his brakes.

Tracy turned to her left just as the car went into a skid and slid sideways across the intersection. The shock of seeing this mass of metal coming right at her momentarily paralyzed Tracy. With her eyes open wide in horror, she stood there, unable to move. Twister barked twice in panic.

When the car hit Tracy, the impact knocked Twister out of her arms and sent the girl flying across the hood. Fortunately, Tracy had enough wits about her to tuck her body and cover her head with her arms. She landed with a sickening thud on the pavement.

For a brief moment, Tracy felt nothing and heard nothing. Then the pain spread out like the cracks of a broken window—first in her head, then her arms, and finally her legs. Startled witnesses poured out of their cars and rushed over to the stricken girl.

"Don't move!" ordered an older man in a business suit. "We'll get you help right away."

"Does someone have a blanket?" asked a woman as the crowd began forming around Tracy.

"Back up, people," said another witness. "Give her room to breathe!"

Tracy's mind reeled from the horror of the accident. *I'm not dead. Is this a nightmare? No, it's real. I hurt all over. This can't be happening to me. Twister! Where's Twister? Oh, please be all right, please, please.*

Despite the pain, Tracy tried to sit up. "My dog, where's my dog?" She groggily gazed around, her eyes frantically searching through the legs of the people in the crowd. And then she spotted him—sprawled motionless on the street about ten feet (3 m) behind the circle of bystanders.

"Somebody, please help my dog." It was the last thing Tracy said before losing consciousness.

* * *

Tracy awoke with a splitting headache. She fluttered her eyes and took a slow and deliberate glance around the dimly lit room. "Where am I? What happened to me?"

"Oh, sweetheart, you're waking up!" her mother said as she gently stroked Tracy's face.

"We're right here with you, honey," said her father. "You're in the hospital. You suffered some injuries, but the doctor says you'll pull through just fine."

Slowly Tracy began to gather her thoughts and remember the horrifying events of the afternoon. "I was hit by a car. Do I have any broken bones?" She looked at her arms and moaned. Both her arms were placed in splints below the elbows. "My legs?" Both her legs were bandaged. She felt her face. A bandage covered the top of her head.

"Your arms are broken, your legs are banged up, and you have a mild concussion," said her mother. "It could have been so much worse. Thank goodness you were wearing knee and elbow pads."

"Twister. What about Twister? Is he okay?" Tracy asked, holding her breath and closing her eyes, hoping the news would be good.

"He's fine," replied her mother, who then glanced at Tracy's father.

"Oh, that's great, just great," said Tracy, letting out a huge sigh of relief. "I was so worried about him. He looked so lifeless out there in the street."

"Now don't talk anymore and get some rest," suggested her father. "The doctor said we could only stay for a few minutes. We'll be here bright and early in the morning."

"I'm so groggy, and I ache all over."

"Goodnight, sweetheart. We love you very much." Her mother leaned over and gave her a kiss as Tracy slipped back into a deep sleep.

* * *

Tracy awoke to the sound of the hospital room door creaking open. She expected to see a nurse, but no one stepped inside. Tracy looked at the clock on the bedside table. It read 4:08 A.M. She was about to doze off when she thought she heard a soft bark. *I must be imagining things,* she told herself. *I could have sworn I heard a dog barking.*

"Ruff."

If I didn't know better, I'd swear that was Twister. It sounds just like him.

"Ruff."

With some effort, Tracy rolled on her side, looked down on the floor, and cried out with delight. Sitting on the floor and wagging his tail was Twister—with his favorite rope toy dangling from his mouth.

"Twister, it's you!" Tracy cried out with joy. "I don't believe it! Are you okay? You look great!" Then, quickly lowering her voice, she whispered, "Oops, I'd better not talk too loudly or the nurse will come in and throw you out."

Tracy beamed and shook her head in awe. "How in the world did you find me? How did you get in here? Leave it to you, Twister. You're one in a million, and I love you for it.

"You brought your loop-de-loop. I wish I could play with you, but . . ." She held up her splinted arms. "As you can see, I don't think I'll be able to play tug-of-war for a few weeks. Come on up here, boy. Let me give you a kiss."

But, strangely, Twister wouldn't jump up on Tracy's bed. He simply wagged his tail and gave a little yelp. "I just can't believe you found me," Tracy said, beaming. "You are absolutely amazing. I wish I could give you a big hug. Come here, boy."

Just then, the nurse peeked in and said to Tracy, "Oh, you're up. I was just checking in on you. How do you feel?"

"Much better— especially with the company I have."

The nurse looked around. "I don't understand. I don't see anyone."

Tracy giggled. "Please don't get mad, but somehow my dog managed to find me and is paying me a visit."

"What? A dog in the hospital? That's impossible. Where is he?" The nurse flicked on the light and glanced around the room. "I don't see any dog."

"Sure he's here. Come here Twister." She waited a moment. "Twister! Come on, boy. It's okay." Still nothing. "That's so weird. He was here just a second ago. You must have heard him. He barked right before you walked in."

"I didn't hear a thing, dear. And I certainly didn't see a dog. I can't imagine how one could get in here anyway. Perhaps you were dreaming about him."

"No, I'm positive. I woke up just a few minutes ago, and he walked into the room. I could see him from the light of the hallway because he opened the door a little bit."

"Dear, I was standing in the doorway, so he couldn't have left without me seeing him. And as you can see, he's not in the room, so . . ."

"It was a dream?" Tracy asked.

"Either that or your mind was playing tricks on you. After all, you did suffer a concussion. It's quite common for accident victims to imagine things."

"It all seemed so real," said Tracy, rubbing her head. "But then, how could Twister have known to come to this hospital and to this room? I guess it couldn't have happened like I thought."

"Try to get some more sleep, dear. Maybe you'll dream about your dog again."

Tracy put her head back on the pillow, but she didn't sleep. She couldn't—because all she could think about was Twister.

About 8 A.M., her parents returned to her room. "Sweetheart, how are you feeling?"

"Much better, Mom," replied Tracy, sitting up in her bed. "Mom, Dad, I had this wild dream that Twister came to visit me during the night. He came right into the room and barked and wagged his tail. So how's he doing?"

Her mother bit her lip, took a deep breath, and reached over to hold Tracy's hand. "Honey, I don't know how to make this easy for you. But Twister died a few hours ago."

The words struck Tracy with the same force as the skidding car. "Died? Died?" she questioned. "But, you said last night that he was fine."

"Honey, forgive me. I told you a white lie then. I just couldn't bear to tell you that he was hurt real badly. We took him to the vet's, but they said there wasn't much hope. We called the animal hospital this morning before coming over here. They said Twister passed away shortly after 4 A.M."

"I can't believe it," murmured Tracy. "Twister dead." Tears began streaming down her face, and she buried her head in her hands. Then suddenly she stopped crying and gulped. "Mom, Dad, I know exactly what time he died! It had to be 4:08. That's what the clock said in my dream when I saw him . . . when I saw him for the last time." Tracy slumped back down on her pillow and sobbed while her parents tried to comfort her.

Later that morning, Tracy got out of bed for the first time since the accident and began shuffling toward the bathroom. As she reached for the doorknob, her foot hit something sticking out from underneath a chair. She looked down and gasped.

"Oh, my gosh!" Tracy said out loud. "It wasn't a dream after all. Twister really *was* here. His ghost came back to say good-bye to me!"

Tracy then reached down and, with a trembling hand, picked up all the proof she needed—Twister's favorite toy, the loop-de-loop.

THE TELL-TALE BONES

For his tenth birthday, Craig Crawford and his father Leonard went camping in a remote area in the lowlands of South Carolina.

They drove west from their home in Charleston out into the country until they passed a few ramshackle houses and empty stores that had been part of a once-bustling little town. They arrived at a clearing beside a pond nestled in a forest thick with graceful cypress trees and towering oaks. The bays, hollies, and magnolias that surrounded the clearing sweetened the air and added a splash of color.

"Man, we're out in the middle of nowhere," said Craig with a whistle as he gazed at the wilderness. "No one will ever find us out here."

Or so he mistakenly thought.

"We're going to have a great time," said Leonard, rubbing his son's short hair.

"Dad, you're not going to turn this trip into a science lecture because you're a biology professor, are you?"

His father laughed. "Why, of course I am. And we'll have fun doing it."

Craig let out a mock groan and then broke into a big smile. Actually, he loved the outdoors and shared his father's appreciation for the beauty and wonders of the environment. So, after pitching their tent, father and son went on a brief hike and then ambled over to the pond with their fishing poles, hoping to catch dinner.

Pointing up a cypress tree at a bird with a yellowish crown of plumes, Craig asked, "What's that, Dad?"

"That's a yellow-crowned night heron, a rather sinister-looking bird. They catch fish, but in a most unusual way. They grasp them in their bills, toss them in the air, and swallow them headfirst."

"Gee, I thought for sure we'd be alone."

"There are hundreds of species of animals out here—"

"No, Dad, I'm talking about humans. Look over there." He pointed toward the other side of the pond. A lanky man in his early twenties stood motionless under a sweat-stained, wide-brimmed, floppy hat. He also wore denim overalls, a dirty white shirt, and knee-high boots. Beside him, gripping a bone in his mouth, sat a white and brown coonhound. They were facing Craig and his father.

Craig waved at them, but they didn't respond. They remained still. Suddenly, a gust blew across the pond at the Crawfords, and they covered their eyes as leaves and dirt swirled around them. When the wind died down a moment later, they looked across the water. The man and his dog were gone.

* * *

That night, after Craig and his father grilled their catch of the day, they sat side by side on a log in front of the fire. "Okay," said Leonard. "Let's be real quiet and see how many night sounds we can identify."

Quank, quank, quank.

"I know, those are tree frogs, right?" asked Craig.

"Very good."

Hoo, hoo, hoo, hoo-hooo-aw.

"Barred owl?"

"Correct again, son."

"And that," Craig said, slapping his forearm, "was a buzzing mosquito."

Craig suddenly noticed that goose pimples covered his arms. The air had become very still and the night noises had ceased. An uncomfortable feeling that they were being watched slowly crept over Craig. While his dad rambled on about the eating habits of the barred owl, Craig slowly looked behind them. His whole body jerked in surprise, and he let out a yelp.

"Craig, what's wrong?" Leonard wheeled around and saw what had startled his son. Standing ten feet (3 m) away were the same man and his dog whom they had seen earlier on the other side of the pond.

The flickering light from the fire danced across the man's pale narrow chin, long slender nose, and high forehead. He had a kindness about him, but his deep-set eyes seemed weary and sad.

His hand rested on the dark brown head of his dog. She had big floppy ears, a cream-colored body with an odd brown marking along her left shoulder, sort of like a leaf. Her thin brown tail wiggled ever so slightly. And clenched between her teeth was a long, shiny white bone.

"Didn't mean to startle you none," said the man.

"We didn't hear you approaching," Leonard remarked. "You took us by surprise."

"Seldom see any campers out here," said the man. "Pretty remote. You two father and son?" They nodded. "That's good."

"Do you live around here?" Craig asked.

The man gave a half-hearted laugh. "Live here? No. Used to. Don't anymore."

Leonard, eyeing the bone in the dog's mouth, asked, "Mind if I take a look at that bone?"

"I don't think she's gonna give it up to a stranger," said the man. "She's a good old hound and minds me. But when it comes to snatching a bone out of her mouth, why, she can be meaner than a poked gator."

The look in Leonard's eyes told Craig that his father didn't feel comfortable being with this man. "Sir," said Leonard, "if you don't mind, we were having a nice father-son talk, and . . ."

"Oh—of course, of course. Didn't mean to disturb you. Have a pleasant time and enjoy your camping." The man and his dog turned and slipped into the darkness. Silently.

"Hey, Dad, what's up?" Craig asked in a hushed tone. "You acted like you had a bad feeling about that guy."

"I can't put my finger on it, Craig. But something bothered me about him. And that dog. I wish I could have gotten a better look at that bone."

"Why?"

The frown on Leonard's face quickly changed to one of his typical smiles. "Oh, it's nothing. Curiosity. You know me, always wanting to examine bones and things. Now where were we? Oh yes, we were listening to night sounds."

* * *

The day after they returned from their camping trip, Leonard sat down at the dinner table with a startling admission. "I didn't want to scare you out there, Craig. But I'm pretty sure the bone that dog was carrying belonged to a human. It was the femur. That's the thigh bone—the one that goes from the hip to the knee. It was clean as a whistle, so I'm assuming that the body the bone came from has been dead for many months or years.

"Wow!" said Craig.

"I talked to Sheriff Wilson about it. He sent a couple of deputies up to the area to see if they can find that man and his dog. They'd like to know where the bone came from."

"Do you think it was murder?"

"Not necessarily. It could be that the dog dug up an old grave. But the bone didn't look *that* old."

A few days later, the sheriff called and told Leonard that the deputies had no luck in finding the man or his dog. The sheriff said, "Since all we have to go on are your suspicions that a dog was carrying a human bone, and since there are no reports of anyone missing in the area, there's nothing more we can do."

* * *

Craig and his father soon forgot about their eerie encounter with the man and his dog—that is, until the following year when they returned to the pond for another camping trip on Craig's eleventh birthday.

"Before turning in for the night, how about roasting some marshmallows?" Leonard suggested.

"Great!" said Craig. "I'll find us some good sturdy sticks." With his flashlight, the boy began scouring the ground a few yards from the campsite when he suddenly came upon a pair of boots. A chill slithered up his spine as Craig gazed from the boots to the overalls, and finally to the face of the sad-eyed young man he had seen at the pond the previous year.

"It's, it's you again," Craig stammered.

"Startled you, huh?" replied the man. "Sorry."

Then the dog appeared by the man's side. Craig gulped. In her mouth was a long white bone—looking like the same one that his dad suspected was human.

"Uh, I've got to go. Bye," said Craig. He turned around and hurried back to the campfire. "Dad, guess what?" he said anxiously. "I just bumped into . . ."

He could tell by his father's expression that the man and his dog were standing behind him.

"How y'all doing," hailed the man. "Apologize for scaring the young one. Me and my hound were just roaming around and caught a glimpse of your campfire."

"Sir," said Leonard, "I'm quite concerned. The last time we met—"

"It was last year," the man interrupted, "on this very date, July 16—"

"How did you know?" asked Leonard. Without waiting for an answer, he continued, "Your dog was carrying a bone exactly like the one he's got in his mouth now. I'm a biologist, and I can tell from here that it's a femur—the femur of a human. Where did he get it?"

The man glanced away and said nothing, appearing to be deep in thought. He took off his hat, revealing a head of thick, curly blond hair. He put his right foot up on a log, leaned forward, and rested his right forearm on his thigh.

"That bone has quite a history behind it. Dates all the way back to 1938. Two farmers, Strom Woodward and Mason Hopkins, had a bitter feud going. They never cared much for each other. Used to duke it out in one of the annual boxing matches held in the town square every Fourth of July. Strom usually won during their teen years. But when they got older, Mason got the better of him and beat him three straight times, the last when they were 23.

"Their rivalry heated up after they both began courting the same girl—Marla Dawson. She was mighty, mighty pretty. Long red wavy hair, and eyes as green as pine trees. Well, the guys finally demanded that Marla make a choice—Strom or Mason. She thought about it long and hard and declared that her heart belonged to Mason.

"Well, this threw Strom into a tizzy, and he wanted to get his revenge. So at the next Fourth of July boxing match, Strom sneaked iron weights in his gloves and beat up on Mason. Strom knocked him down three or four times, but Mason kept getting up and battling back. Even though Strom cheated, Mason wound up winning with a right hook to the jaw that knocked him out cold.

"Afterwards, Strom was spitting mad. He'd lost the boxing match, his pride, and his girlfriend. After two weeks, his anger consumed all his rational thought. He grabbed his shotgun and hid out in the brush, waiting to ambush Mason.

"Late one afternoon Mason and his dog—a big old she-hound named Hickory—strolled by. Hickory stopped, sniffed the air, and growled. She smelled trouble and knew Strom was in the bushes up to no good." The man's voice faltered. He swallowed hard, cleared his throat, and then continued. "Strom pulled the trigger and shot the dog dead. Mason cried out, dropped to his knees, and held his dying dog. And then Strom shot Mason in the head and killed him too."

The man's sad eyes flared with anger, and his tone turned to one of disgust. "Strom loaded Mason's body and the dead dog into his truck and drove over to this here pond. He weighed down Mason's body with some rocks, rolled it into the pond, and figured no one would ever find it. Then he buried the dog in a shallow grave.

"The next day, Strom lied to Marla. He told her that Mason said he had to go away for a while, because his grandparents in Cincinnati were ill and needed him to help take care of their farm.

"Strom thought he got away with murder. But he didn't. That night, when he stepped outside his cabin, he was scared out of his boots. There was Hickory, just a-howling and a-yelping and a-growling at him. 'Dog!' he exclaimed. 'You're supposed to be dead! Now get out of here!' Strom ran inside, loaded his shotgun, and then flung open the door. But the dog had high-tailed it out of there.

"The next night, when Strom walked outside to the outhouse, why there was Hickory again. A-barking and a-growling because he knew what Strom had done. 'I don't believe this!' Strom shouted. 'Wait til I get you, you mangy mutt. I'll kill you for sure this time!' He got his shotgun. This time he quietly opened the window. The dog was still barking like crazy, so Strom got a bead on her and blasted away. But Hickory was still yapping.

"Now Strom always had a keen eye. With a rifle, he could shoot a half dollar out of your hand from 100 paces away. He knew he hadn't missed hitting that dog, especially with a shotgun. But darn if that hound just kept on barking at him. So Strom rushed outside and started chasing Hickory until she just took off and disappeared.

"This went on every day after sundown. No sooner would Strom step out of his house than that dog would hound him. By now, Strom was beginning to wonder if maybe, just maybe, this wasn't a real dog. That what was bugging him was a real ghost. Either that or he was going nuts.

"So Strom decided to leave the area for awhile. Thought maybe that would give him some peace. He stayed with friends two counties over from here, but it didn't do any good. The first night there, Hickory showed up and barked at him. The others heard her too. And they saw her. They tried to catch her on account of she was keeping them from their sleep too, but she'd just vanish. In Strom's mind that proved he wasn't plum crazy—he was dealing with an honest-to-goodness ghost.

"Since running away didn't help, Strom returned to his cabin. But he couldn't sleep because of the barking and snarling going on all night long, every night. Strom got so desperate he stuck candle wax in his ears and covered his head with his pillow to drown out the barking.

"But Hickory's haunting was taking a toll on Strom. He was losing weight, couldn't eat much, and barely got enough sleep to get him through the day.

"A couple of months went by. Marla was getting mighty worried because she hadn't heard a word from Mason. She knew that something was wrong, or why else wouldn't he have written or called or sent a telegram.

"Although Strom was still getting tormented by the ghost dog every night, and he was looking poorly, he wouldn't crack. No sir. He kept on as though nothing had happened.

"Well, wouldn't you know, one night Hickory didn't come by his house, and Strom actually got a peaceful sleep. 'Finally, I outlasted that terror of a hound,' he told himself. But he was wrong—dead wrong.

"That night, Hickory came trotting into town carrying a bone in her mouth. She dropped it off in the middle of the town square. No one paid much attention at first. But the next night she does the same thing with another bone. She doesn't bury it or anything. Just leaves it there and barks and then walks off.

"Someone finally says, 'That sure looks like Mason's hound. I wonder if he's back.' The third night, there was a crowd waiting. Hickory came with a big old bone in her mouth, and she dropped it on the grass. Someone finally had the smarts to study the three bones and announced, 'Hey, these aren't no hog bones. They're *people* bones!'

"Needless to say, the townsfolk were shocked. The dog began barking, and the people said, 'Let's follow her and see where she's getting these bones.' So they grabbed some lanterns and ran after Hickory, and she led them to this here pond. She went to the edge and then stepped right in, went under the water, and came up with another bone!

"The sheriff and his men pulled out a lot more bones. Not all the bones, but quite a few. They even found a skull that had been shattered by a gun. They could tell the bones had belonged to a man in his twenties who stood about 6 feet (1.8 m) tall and had once broken his arm. That description fit none other than Mason Hopkins.

"By then the sheriff had a pretty good idea about who killed Mason. So he decided to pay Strom Woodward a visit. But Hickory beat him to it. Strom was sitting on his front porch, strumming on his banjo when he caught sight of that pesky hound. She was carrying a bone in her mouth and walked up, pretty as you please, to Strom and dropped it right at his feet. Strom was so flabbergasted he couldn't even move. His mouth dropped open and his banjo fell onto the porch floor.

"Soon the sheriff drove up and started asking Strom a whole bunch of questions. Strom just mumbled. And then the sheriff spotted the bone and asked, 'Where did you get this?' And Strom said, 'I don't know nothing about it. Some old dog dropped it off.' Then Hickory began barking out back, so the sheriff went over and saw a hole had been dug up. And guess what he found in the hole? More bones!

"The sheriff determined they were from Mason's body. The hound had taken a few of them out of the pond and buried them in Strom's yard. Well, Strom was so shook up he slumped against the side of his house and began to cry. He was blubbering, and no one could understand a word he said. Finally, they got him to calm down so they could make out what he was saying. And Strom confessed, 'I did it! I did it! I killed Mason Hopkins. I shot him in the head, and I tied rocks to his body and tossed him in the pond.

"'That dog of his—I killed her too—came back as a ghost and haunted me. She followed me, and I couldn't get her to shut up. And now I see she's been burying some of Mason's bones in my yard. I can't take it anymore. She's driving me crazy!'

"They sent Strom away to the penitentiary for the rest of his life for murdering Mason."

* * *

"Wow! What a story!" Craig exclaimed. "So what happened to the ghost dog?"

"Legend has it that Hickory and her master sometimes wander these woods together on the anniversary of their death." The man's eyes grew misty. He took a deep breath and said softly, "Didn't mean to take up so much time. Best be leaving now." He turned around, tapped his dog on the head, and mumbled, "Come on, Hickory, let's go." They walked silently into the night.

Craig wasn't sure that he heard right. "Hey, wait a second!" he shouted. "Don't leave!" Then, without catching his breath, Craig turned to his father and whispered excitedly, "Dad, did he just call his dog 'Hickory'?"

Leonard, who had been deep in thought, suddenly rose to his feet and exclaimed, "That's it! That's the brown marking on the dog's left shoulder. It's shaped like a leaf from a hickory tree! I've been trying to figure out what it

34

reminded me of. A hickory leaf, of course."

"Dad, if that dog's name is Hickory, you don't suppose—"

"What? That we were just visited by the ghosts of Mason Hopkins and Hickory?" His father scoffed and shook his head. "Don't be ridiculous."

* * *

For days Craig couldn't stop thinking about the encounter with the man and his dog. Leonard tried to set his son straight. "Look, Craig, that man told a tall tale, okay? There are no such things as ghosts. He probably made up the whole story about that murder."

"But what about the bone the dog was carrying? You said it was human."

"Yes, it definitely was human. But, as I told you before, it probably came from an old grave."

"Isn't there some way we could find out if there really was a murder back then?"

"Well, I suppose we could look at back issues of the local newspaper and see what was written about it—that is, if it ever happened."

The next day, they went to the library to scan microfilm of old issues of the newspaper. "The man told us that Strom was arrested a couple of months after the murder, which supposedly took place sometime after July 4, 1938," said Leonard. "So let's start with the September issues." They loaded the microfilm machine and stared, frame by frame, at the screen. They read about the army of a German madman named Hitler invading the country of Austria, a civil war raging in Spain, Congress passing a law banning child labor, and the New York Yankees whipping the Chicago Cubs in four straight games to win the World Series.

As fatigue set in, Craig and his father cast their eyes upon the front page of the October 25, 1938, issue. The headline read:

MAN CONFESSES TO MURDER
Dog Finds Bones of Victim
Missing for Three Months

Exactly as the man in the woods had told them, the story said that Strom Woodward had been arrested for the murder of Mason Hopkins after Mason's dog Hickory led authorities to the victim's bones.

"It's true," said Leonard. "It's all true!"

"And look," Craig said excitedly. "The story says Mason and the dog were killed July 16. Remember what the man said to us about the ghosts of Mason and Hickory? That they appear near the pond on the anniversary of their death? We were there the last two years—on my birthday, July 16!"

"Son, all that means is the man we met was telling the truth about the murder. But there's no proof of any ghosts. This guy probably gets his kicks by roaming around the area, telling people the story. Let's read on. The article continues on the next page."

Leonard advanced the microfilm. What both of them saw on page two left them limp and speechless.

· Beside the story was a photo with a caption that read, "Murder victim Mason Hopkins and his faithful dog Hickory, taken 12 days before his murder."

Above the caption was a picture of the very same man who had twice visited Craig and his father at their campsite. And by his side, in the photo, was a brown and white hound dog with a distinctive brown spot on his left shoulder shaped exactly like a leaf from a hickory tree.

THE SPIRIT OF MORGAN'S WOODS

One summer afternoon, with the sun slipping behind a ridge of the nearby Smoky Mountains, Wade Hampton and his brother Scott went horseback riding in the area's spookiest forest, Morgan's Woods.

For generations, the forest had been the site of eerie events. People claimed to have seen the ghost of a Civil War soldier wandering around the trees, looking for his lost infantry unit. Others reported hearing unearthly voices crying out in pain. But no one had seen or heard anything ghostly in years—until the Hampton boys arrived.

Wade, 14, and Scott, 13, were spending their summer vacation on the cattle and horse ranch of Uncle Jeb and Aunt Faye in eastern Tennessee. The boys were excellent horsemen and rode every chance they got. Wade sat atop a dark brown saddle horse called Popeye, who got his name because his cheeks would puff out when the bit was placed in his mouth. Scott rode a brown, spirited saddle horse named Rebel.

The boys were talking about the fun they were having on their vacation when Popeye and Rebel unexpectedly started acting up. They both whinnied and stomped their feet. Their heads bobbed up and down.

"Something's bothering the horses," said Wade.

"Maybe there's a wild hog out there," Scott added. "They can get pretty nasty."

The ears of both horses twitched forward—a sure sign that they were frightened.

Leaning over his mount's neck, Wade soothingly told Popeye, "Calm down, boy. It's all right." Wade scanned the woods, looking for the animal or person that was scaring the horses. Popeye, his eyes getting wider, neighed even louder and pawed at the ground.

Beside him, Rebel reared up and backed away while Scott struggled to maintain control. "Hey, Reb, stop it!" Scott commanded.

"Whatever is out there sure has the horses spooked," said Wade.

"What do you think we should do?" asked his brother.

Before Wade could answer, Scott let out a shout. "Look, through the trees! What's that?"

Wade turned to his right and caught a glimpse of a bright white animal about 200 yards (182 m) away, darting through the trees before it quickly disappeared in the lush forest. "What was that?" he asked.

"I don't know. A deer maybe?"

"I've never heard of an all-white deer," said Wade.

"Besides, it seemed bigger than a deer. Let's go see if we can find out what it is."

The horses didn't want any part of going deeper into the woods. Normally obedient, both horses tried to stand their ground and protested their riders' commands to move forward.

"I've never seen Popeye act like this," said Wade.

"Rebel is really putting up a struggle too. That animal definitely bugged them. Let's turn back."

"Before we do, I want to mark this place so we can come back tomorrow and look for tracks. I want to find out what it was."

Wade got off his horse, collected about six sticks, and stood them against each other, forming a waist-high teepee off the side of the path they had been following.

The next day, the boys finished their chores quickly and then hopped on their horses and headed into Morgan's Woods. After finding his marker, Wade said, "The animal we saw was about 200 yards (182 m) away from us off to the right. Let's see if we can find those tracks."

The horses didn't protest this time, and a few moments later the boys reached the spot where they had last seen the eerie white animal. They hopped off their mounts and studied the ground, looking for clues. They found tracks for deer and raccoons, but nothing else unusual until . . .

"Hey, Wade, look at this," shouted Scott.

In the soft dirt along the banks of a stream, they found the print of a horseshoe. "It looks like it was nothing more than a horse heading across the creek," said Wade.

"It sure was a *bright* one," Scott added. "It seemed to glow in the shade."

They forded the stream by hopping from one rock to another until they got to the other side. "Here are some more horseshoe prints," said Wade. He followed them for a bit and then said, "Whoa! Scott look at this!"

Scott ambled over and examined the ground. "I don't see anything."

"That's the point. Look at the prints over there," said Wade, pointing to the hoofprints leading from the stream. "They're heading straight ahead for about 10 yards (9 m). Then they just disappear. If the horse had turned away, we'd have seen tracks off to the left or the right because the ground is still soft. But there aren't any."

"Did the horse just vanish into thin air?"

"That doesn't make much sense," said Wade, "but I can't come up with a better explanation."

The boys went back to the other side of the stream and looked to see where the hoofprints came from. To their surprise, they discovered the prints began about 20 yards (18 m) from the stream. But none before that.

"It's like the horse just came out of nowhere, ran across the creek in front of us, and then went to nowhere," said Scott, scratching his head.

"Well, we know one thing," said Wade. "The horse is not wild. It has horseshoes. That means it must belong to somebody."

* * *

That night at dinner, the brothers told their aunt and uncle about the hoofprints of the strange white horse.

"I don't know of anyone around these parts who owns a white horse," said Uncle Jeb. "Your story sounds pretty unusual to me. But then, you were in Morgan's Woods."

"Now, Jeb," said Aunt Faye. "Don't go and get them all scared up."

"I'm not, Faye. Besides, they're old enough. I can't help it if people say those woods are haunted. Just because you and I haven't ever seen any ghosts there doesn't mean they don't exist."

Turning to the boys, Aunt Faye said, "Maybe you should stay away from the woods—especially at night."

Wade broke out in a grin. "Why, Aunt Faye, you don't believe in ghosts, do you?"

* * *

About a week later, the Hampton brothers had finished their early morning chores and were riding their horses in the woods. Fog covered the valley, fingering through the gaps between the rolling foothills.

The boys returned to the stream near where they had spotted the white horse. They planned to build a makeshift fishing hole by damming up the creek with small trees that they were going to chop down.

Just as Wade was about to swing his axe at a sycamore tree, the horses, who had been quietly munching on ground cover a few yards away, whinnied with alarm. They began backing up and stomping their feet.

"Something is out there," said Wade. "Better get our horses."

But as the boys approached them, the steeds took off in fright. "Hey, Popeye, get back here!"

"Rebel! Whoa! Come back!"

The horses had fled into the morning mist. "What's going

on here?" wondered Wade.

"Wade, look behind you!"

Wade turned around. Out of the fog galloped a dazzling white stallion. He held his long head high like a king, and his flowing mane fluttered majestically in the breeze. His large nostrils flared wide. A bold black mark streaked down his neck and stopped midway at his muscular chest.

"Look out!" shouted Wade. "He's heading right for us!"

Both boys began to scramble when Scott tripped and fell and sprawled face first onto the ground. Wade turned around and, fearing that his brother would be trampled, rushed back to help. He reached Scott with only enough time for both of them to roll up into balls, cover their heads, and hope they wouldn't get stomped.

They braced themselves against the deadly hoofs, but nothing happened. Wade poked up his head and looked around.

"Where's the horse?" asked Scott.

"He's gone!"

"But he was heading right toward us. Where did he go?"

The shaken boys got to their feet and looked around. "The tracks!" shouted Wade. "Look at the tracks! They end about five feet (1.5 m) from where we were."

"They don't veer off or anything. He just disappeared like that," said Scott, snapping his fingers. "This is getting freaky. Come on, let's get out of here."

The boys whistled for their horses and eventually found them about a quarter mile (.4 km) away. When the boys returned to the barn, they excitedly recounted their brush with the mysterious white stallion to Wiley Pickett, one of the old ranch hands.

He stopped brushing the horse he was grooming, took off his grimy cowboy hat, and rubbed his stubbly chin. "Did this horse have a dark black streak running from his throat down to his chest?"

"He sure did," said Wade. "Do you know who he is?"

"Sounds like Alabaster to me."

"Whose horse is he?" asked Scott.

"Well, he probably belongs to Winfield Morgan."

"Does Winfield Morgan have anything to do with Morgan's Woods?" Wade asked.

Wiley nodded. "He's *the* Morgan."

"But I thought Morgan was some guy who lived back in the 1800s," said Scott.

Wiley nodded again. "That he was."

"Wait a second," said Wade. "Are you saying that the horse we saw is owned by a guy who lived in the last century?"

"That I am," Wiley replied.

"You're pulling our legs," Scott claimed. "Horses don't live that long."

"Who says he's alive?" asked Wiley, raising one bushy brown eyebrow.

"Now you're joshing us for sure," declared Wade.

"Not true, boys. I'm guessing that what you saw was the ghost of Alabaster, Winfield Morgan's pride and joy."

The boys looked at each other and grinned. They were convinced that Wiley was putting them on, but they figured it wouldn't hurt to listen to the old man spin a yarn about a ghostly steed.

Wiley leaned on a stable door, pulled out a hand-carved

toothpick, and began picking at his teeth. "Let me tell you about Winfield Morgan. He was a pretty rich man back in the 1800s. He owned much of the land around here and raised cattle and horses. He watched over his huge spread while riding on his prized steed, a magnificent white horse called Alabaster—named after a kind of white rock that's used to make statues and vases.

"Morgan and Alabaster were a familiar sight as they made their way across his land. Although there was plenty of pasture, they liked to spend time deep in the woods where Morgan could think.

"Even though he had lots of cattle, horses, acres, and money, the thing Morgan cherished the most were the trees in his forest—beech, elm, hickory, oak, and sycamore. Acre after acre, thousands of them, were permitted to grow as wild woodland because that was the way he wanted it.

"Morgan loved those trees so much that he ordered all his workers never to cut down a single one without his permission. He would examine the trees from atop Alabaster, marking those that he would allow to be cut down. To him, each tree was an individual with its own personality. He considered them living, breathing creatures needing his care and protection.

"If someone dared try to chop down a tree—even for firewood—he and Alabaster would charge at the person and run him off the land."

The boys looked at each other in amazement. "Wiley," said Scott. "We were just about to cut down a tree when that horse came out of nowhere!"

"See? There you are. Alabaster felt a kinship with the forest. In fact, he sometimes acted jittery in the open spaces. But in the woods he seemed to shine. His white coat lit up the entire forest."

"The horse looked like it was glowing!" Scott exclaimed.

"I believe it," said Wiley, moving the toothpick to the corner of his mouth. "Now, where was I? Oh, yes, when the Civil War was heading toward a climax in 1864, life turned sour for Morgan. The Union troops were sweeping through the countryside, destroying everything in sight to break the spirit as well as the back of the Confederates. The Yankees stole most everything they could take from farmers and burned the rest.

"When the bluecoats arrived at Morgan's huge ranch, he greeted them from his front porch, hoping if he acted nice they'd leave him alone. Not a chance. They were convinced he had stashed a fortune in gold, and they demanded to know where he hid it. He denied that he had any, and stubbornly refused to talk further about it. So they threatened to burn down his barn if he didn't tell them where the gold was buried. When he remained silent, they torched the barn.

"As the barn burned, the soldiers set out on their own and headed into the woods, along the paths that Morgan and Alabaster had traveled on. They stuck their bayonets into the ground at spots where they thought the gold might be hidden. But they didn't find any at first.

"The soldiers went deeper and deeper into the woods when suddenly they heard the whinny of a horse. They followed the sound until it led them to a clearing in a remote part of the forest. There, they found a beautiful white horse—Alabaster—tied to a tree. Morgan had left him there with a good supply of water and hay, hoping to keep him from the Yankees.

"But Alabaster, hearing the soldiers' horses in the

distance, had innocently called out to them. His neighing had given away his hiding place. The Yankees then snooped around and, lo and behold, they found Morgan's gold, hidden under a bale of hay. The soldiers grabbed the gold and then led Alabaster back to the ranch.

"Morgan pleaded with the soldiers. They could keep the gold, he said, but please let him keep Alabaster. He loved that horse as much as he did the trees. But Alabaster was too fine a horse for the soldiers to give up. The last Morgan saw of Alabaster, he was whinnying and quivering under a rider in a blue uniform. Alabaster turned one last time and looked wide-eyed and sad at Morgan. The poor horse knew he had mistakenly betrayed himself and his master.

"Morgan was so upset that he pulled out a pistol he had hidden under a floorboard on the porch and shot the rider. The soldiers then returned fire and killed Morgan."

"What happened to Alabaster?" asked Scott.

"They say he died of a broken heart a short time after Morgan's death. His spirit returned to the woods, protecting the trees and searching for his master."

The brothers sat quietly for a moment before Wade said, "That was a great tale, Wiley."

"That's no tale, son. That's the truth."

"Have you ever seen Alabaster's ghost?" asked Scott.

"Nope. I haven't heard of anyone seeing him since I was knee-high to a piglet. Until you saw him today."

* * *

During the last month of their vacation, the boys went out to Morgan's Woods six more times, but they never saw the strange white horse.

Two days before the end of their vacation, Wade went for a ride alone with Popeye. He told his aunt he was heading to a nearby lake. But on the way there, he spotted a gliding eagle and followed it until it came to rest atop a tree in Morgan's Woods.

Suddenly, Popeye let out a startled neigh. Wade heard the unmistakable sound of an angry rattlesnake. He looked down and saw that his horse had been bitten in the front right leg by the deadly reptile. Popeye then reared up so high and fast that Wade flipped backward over the horse's rump. The boy crashed into a large rock, shoulder first.

The moment he landed hard on the ground, Wade heard a sickening snap in his left leg and felt a jabbing pain. He knew he was badly injured. He later learned that he had broken not only his leg but also his collarbone and several ribs. The pain grew so intense that he passed out.

When Wade regained consciousness, he tried to sit up, but his injuries hurt too much. Luckily, the snake had slithered away. Wade breathed with difficulty and could utter only a weak moan because of his broken ribs. *I hurt so much,* Wade thought. *I can't walk. I can't shout. No one knows I'm out here. I told Aunt Faye I was going to ride around the lake. They won't think to look here in the woods. Maybe Popeye headed back to the barn. That's what horses usually do when they don't have a rider. At least then people will know something has happened to me, and they'll start a search. But it might take forever before they think to look for me in Morgan's Woods. Still, it's my only hope.*

Just then he heard a snort. *That sounds like a horse. Is it Popeye? Or a searcher?* Weakly, Wade tried again to sit up.

Despite the pain in his shoulder and ribs, he managed to peek over the rock. *Oh, no! It's Popeye and he's hurt!*

Several yards away his horse lay on his side, breathing heavily. His right front leg was swollen and shaky.

Wade slumped back down. *It will be nightfall before they realize I'm missing. They won't be able to start a search until morning. This pain, it's so bad.*

He began to feel dizzy and was slowly losing consciousness again when suddenly he heard the snorting and neighing of a horse. He lifted his head just enough to see that it wasn't Popeye. It was the mysterious white horse, rearing up on its hind legs and pawing at the air.

"Alabaster?" said the dazed boy. Then he passed out again.

* * *

"Wiley, over here!" shouted Uncle Jeb, as he pulled on the reins of his horse. "It's Popeye! He's hurt! Wade must be around here somewhere. Wade? Wade, where are you?"

Wade, trying to clear his foggy head, feebly yelled, "Over here! Behind the rock!"

Uncle Jeb jumped off his horse and ran over to the injured boy. "Wade! Are you all right?"

"Uncle Jeb, am I glad to see you! I think I broke my leg. My ribs hurt too."

"What happened?"

"A rattlesnake bit Popeye, and he threw me. I landed on a rock. Is Popeye dead?"

"No, but he's in bad shape." Turning to Wiley, Jeb barked, "Get back to the ranch. Call the medics and get them over here with a stretcher. We've got a badly injured boy. Then call Doc Sanders at the animal hospital. Tell him we need him to treat a horse with a snakebite. And *hurry!*"

"Uncle Jeb," Wade said groggily, "is it morning?"

"No, it's about 5 P.M. Why?"

"How did you find me so fast? No one knew I was out here. With Popeye laid up, I figured no one would know I was in trouble."

"We didn't know. It's the darnedest thing. About a half hour ago, Wiley and I were on our horses, checking the herd, when this white stallion came galloping out of Morgan's Woods and headed straight toward us. Spooked the living daylights out of the cows and the horses. We were pretty stunned too, because we had never seen him before.

"Well, he kept rearing up and snorting and whinnying to beat the band. He ran from one end of the fence line to the other. We just stood there and watched. But then he seemed to get angry. He began kicking at the fence and knocked a section down. That got my dander up. So Wiley and I hopped on our horses and took off after him. He led us into Morgan's Woods. The weirdest thing was that he wasn't that far ahead of us. Yet at least three times he seemed to disappear and then reappear. The last time we saw him was right near where Popeye is lying. That's when I discovered you."

"Did the horse have a black mark running down his chest?"

"I believe he did."

"That's the horse Scott and I saw! That was Alabaster. Uncle Jeb, I just got saved by the ghost of a white stallion!"

BINGO'S SECRET

Alex Hammond walked up to the gray granite tombstone and bent over to read the inscription.

RANDALL BARON STEVENS
Born February 22, 1951
Died August 5, 1959

"So this is where he's buried," said the 15-year-old boy.

"Yes," replied Aunt Suzy, gazing at the grave with a bittersweet look of sadness and fondness. "It took a long time for your grandparents, your mother, and I to get over Randy's death. Our little brother was so young, so loved."

She kneeled down and pulled out a dandelion and several weeds that had sprouted on the grass over the grave. "In a way, Bingo played a part in easing our pain," she said. "The love that collie shared with Randy was absolutely incredible.

Those two were inseparable—in life and in death."

"And no one knows about Bingo's secret?"

"No one but our immediate family. And we want to keep it that way."

* * *

Alex first learned of the secret a few months earlier from his mother Debbie, the older sister of Randy and Suzy.

In 1953, Debbie's parents, John and Barbara Stevens, bought Randy a collie puppy for his second birthday. They named the dog Bingo, after the family's favorite game. The collie sported a soft wispy coat of snowy white and golden brown—and the strangest bark anyone had ever heard. It sounded like a cross between an old man's cough and a hoarse coyote.

Bingo got along fine with the girls and their two cats, but it was clear from the start that he was Randy's dog—and lifesaver.

Bingo became a hero a year after he arrived. Randy had been taking a nap with his mother when he woke up and walked out the back door. The three-year-old boy was wandering away from home. When Bingo saw him leave the yard, the collie dashed after him and stayed by his side. Bingo whined, sensing that maybe it wasn't a good idea to be going off like this. But he was a loyal dog who wanted to be with his boy.

About a quarter mile (.4 km) away, they came to a highway. Seeing a shiny coin in the middle of the road, Randy walked out to pick it up, paying absolutely no attention to the traffic. But Bingo did. The collie ran circles around the boy and began barking as cars in each direction screeched to a halt. The motorists wondered if they had been stopped by a mad dog.

Bingo stood in the center of the road, blocking cars and even leaping against their fenders to keep them from creeping forward. Just a few feet away sat Randy, innocently playing on the pavement.

Motorists looked on in wonder as the dog rushed back to the child and nudged him to the shoulder of the road. But the little boy, thinking it was a game, scurried back to the center of the highway and plopped down, laughing. Finally, a police officer cautiously approached the worried dog and calmed him down so the officer could pick up Randy and carry him to safety.

Ever since then, Bingo became extra protective of his master. Part of the reason was because Randy was a frail, often sickly kid—but one who seldom complained and always smiled.

The two did everything together—they played, slept, and sometimes even ate together. Once a week, on Saturday mornings, Randy and Bingo shared breakfast while watching cartoons on TV. Randy would fix two bowls of cereal and take them to the family room, where Bingo was already stretched out in front of the television set.

"Okay, let's eat," said Randy. He would sit down on the floor, put one bowl in his lap, and place the other near his dog. Bingo would wag his tail and then slide slowly on his stomach toward the bowl on the floor. While Randy slurped his cereal, the collie would carefully lap up the milk and cereal from his bowl.

Bingo soon outweighed Randy, growing to more than 100

pounds (45 kg). The collie displayed a big heart and an even greater understanding for Randy's physical limitations. The dog was patient with his undersized, often-tired master and was careful never to play too rough with him.

Whenever they played in the backyard, Bingo would race across the lawn and charge after Randy as if to bowl him over, only to change direction at the last instant and leap past him. Sometimes, to show his impish side, the collie would sneak up behind Randy and playfully push him to the ground. Randy would start laughing and then roll around with his dog.

When Randy was five years old and in kindergarten, Bingo often trotted over to the school yard, just to keep an eye on his master. During recess, when the kids were at the playground, Bingo stood watch to make sure that no harm came to Randy, that no bully shoved him. But the dog didn't need to worry because everyone liked Randy. And they especially liked Bingo, who patiently let kids hug and kiss him.

In second grade, Randy kept getting sicker, so his parents took him to a specialist who ran many tests. When the results came back, the family's worst fears were realized. Randy was dying of leukemia—cancer of the blood. Back then, there wasn't much doctors could do for such patients. It was only a matter of time before Randy would die.

Despite the death sentence, Randy kept his spirits up and hoped for the best. It helped having his best friend, Bingo, by his side.

Although Bingo loved being outside, he chose to stay with Randy in his room, because the dog sensed his master could use the company. On Randy's good days—which were few and far between—Bingo would pick up an old red rubber ball and place it on the bed. Randy would throw it so Bingo could fetch it. The bedroom was small, but the collie didn't mind because he was playing with his master.

Then there were the bad days—days when Randy was too weak to do much more than give his dog a few pats on the head. But the collie never complained. He'd jump up on the bed, scoot over to Randy's hand, and lick it, just to let the boy know that his pal loved him.

Soon came the moment that Randy dreaded—when he had to go to the hospital to live out his final days. Before leaving the house for the last time, the bedridden boy whispered for his dog to come over. Bingo walked up to the bed and rested his head on the mattress next to Randy's shoulder and looked lovingly at his master.

"Bingo," Randy whispered, "I have to go away for awhile. I need you to help take care of things, okay? With me gone, the girls in our family will outnumber us boys, so I'm counting on you to help out and be good. But you've always been good. You're the best dog a boy could ever have. Why, you're the best dog in the whole world. Now listen, make sure you wake up Suzy and Debbie every Saturday morning and have them get you a bowl of cereal, okay? I've got to go now. Good-bye, Bingo. I love you."

Bingo barked that distinctive odd bark of his and then licked the boy's face long and hard.

Over the next few days, Bingo seldom ate as he moped around the house. He and Randy had never been separated for more than a day or two. So without Randy, Bingo felt lost. He kept going into Randy's room, lying on his bed, and going out only occasionally when the girls pleaded with him to play. He fetched and chased and rough-housed with them—but his heart wasn't in it.

When Randy's health took a turn for the worse, John and Barbara began a bedside vigil at the hospital. Back home, Randy's sisters had just gone to bed under the watchful eye of Mrs. O'Malley, the next-door neighbor and babysitter. She turned on the radio, settled into the easy chair, and began working on her needlepoint.

Suddenly, Bingo, who had been curled up on Randy's empty bed, let out a heart-stopping wail. He leapt to the floor, ran into Randy's closet, grabbed a shoe, and darted into the living room. He shook his head from side to side and let the shoe fly across the room while Mrs. O'Malley looked on in bewilderment.

The dog barked and whined, ran around the room like he didn't know what to do, and then tore into Randy's room again. He snatched a shirt off the hanger and dragged it back into the living room where he whimpered and howled.

The commotion woke up the girls. "What's going on?" asked Debbie. "Why is Bingo acting so weird?"

"I don't know," Mrs. O'Malley replied. "Has he ever done this before?"

"No," said Suzy. "Look, now he's got Randy's cap."

The collie kept picking up and throwing Randy's clothes around the room and making whimpering noises that the girls had never heard before. They tried to comfort him, but he would break free, pick up an item, fling it, and then whine.

Bingo finally calmed down after 15 minutes of anguish and went back into Randy's room.

An hour later, Randy's parents came home, their faces drained and their eyes red. Without a word being spoken, Mrs. O'Malley knew instantly what had happened. Randy had died. She threw her arms around both grieving parents and joined them in a long cry.

"He was such a good little boy," sighed Barbara. "He loved everyone and, oh, how he loved that dog of his."

"Bingo!" exclaimed Mrs. O'Malley. "He went crazy tonight. He pulled Randy's things out of the bedroom and dragged them in here, howling and barking."

"When did this happen?" asked Barbara.

"A little over an hour ago, about 9:30."

Barbara turned to her husband and squeezed his hand hard. "John, that's when Randy died. You don't think that Bingo somehow knew and that's why he carried on so crazily?"

"The way those two loved each other . . . I wouldn't doubt it for a moment," he replied.

Two days later, the tearful Stevens family and many friends and relatives attended a graveside funeral service and buried Randy in Hillside Memorial Cemetery. Among the mourners was the ever faithful Bingo, his head bowed and tail drooped.

When the funeral was over, Bingo refused to leave the grave where his master's coffin had been lowered. "Come on, Bingo, it's time to go," John said softly, gently stroking the sad dog. Bingo didn't even look up. His eyes remained fixed on the grave. "Bingo, we have to go now. Come on, boy."

"Let him be, John," said Barbara. "Maybe he needs to have some time alone with Randy. Bingo will come home when he's ready. Besides, the house isn't that far away from here."

But by dinner, Bingo had yet to return. As night fell, John got into the car and drove to the cemetery, looking for the collie. He found Bingo milling around the grave site. John got out of the car, walked up to the dog, and kneeled down. "Hi, Bingo. Are you okay, boy? You really miss Randy, don't you? We all do. He was a great kid." For the next half hour, John sat on the ground with Bingo and talked about his son, reliving all the good times and even the few bad ones. The talk helped ease the ache in John's heart—and, it seemed, in Bingo's.

"Hey, we better get going now, okay?" said John. When the dog whimpered, John gently grabbed him by the collar and said, "It's okay. Randy understands. We need to go home now and get you some food and water." Reluctantly, the dog left the cemetery.

But Bingo refused to eat—even when Barbara cooked him a hamburger and put it in his food dish. That night, the dog slept on Randy's bed. At dawn, the collie was scratching at the back door, barking to be let out. Suzy, the first one up, sleepily opened the door, and Bingo charged outside. He streaked through Mrs. O'Malley's yard, cut across the park, and scampered down the sidewalk to the cemetery.

When he arrived at Randy's grave, Bingo lay down with his paws outstretched in the front, just like he used to do when he and Randy would watch Saturday morning cartoons.

And so began the vigil.

* * *

Every day for the next month, Bingo arrived at the crack of dawn and spent the entire day by Randy's grave. He took naps there, walked around, and kept the squirrels away. The groundskeepers didn't annoy him. In fact, they often gave him scraps of food from their lunch pails, but he seldom ate anything.

As the days passed, the dog grew weaker. When he returned home at night, he would take a mouthful of water and a few bites of dog food and then go into Randy's room—which the parents had left exactly as it was when their son was alive.

Worried about Bingo's health, Barbara and John took him to the vet's. But the doctor couldn't find anything physically wrong, except that the collie was losing weight from lack of eating. "Here, give him some vitamins. Mix it up with his food and feed him by hand if you have to," the vet told them. "If you don't force him to eat, he may not last very long."

But despite the best efforts of the Stevens family, Bingo rejected all food other than what John almost forced down the dog's throat.

A week after his visit to the vet's, Bingo, now just a shell of his former self, barked weakly to be let out early one chilly damp morning. His once bright, fluffy, white and tan coat had taken on a dull luster. His proud head hung low and his high-stepping gait had been replaced by a slow walk.

He never came home.

They found Bingo lying on his side atop Randy's grave with his right paw touching the gravestone of his young master.

One of the gravediggers called John at home and broke the news to him. John and Barbara, heartbroken over Bingo's death, went to the cemetery.

"What a wonderful, loyal dog," said John, as his eyes welled with tears. "He refused to be separated from Randy. Such devotion . . ." He was too choked up to finish his sentence.

"John, do you know what Randy would want more than anything?" asked Barbara. "He'd want to have Bingo buried right next to him."

"You're right. He'd love that. Let's do it."

But when they asked permission, the cemetery director was shocked. "A dog? Buried *here?* I'm sorry, but that's not possible. This cemetery is for humans only. It's totally against the rules."

So the Stevens brought Bingo's body home, where John dug a big hole in the backyard under a tall elm tree. Barbara took Randy's bedspread, which Bingo had always slept on, and wrapped him in it. After they placed his body in the hole, John, Barbara, and the two girls held hands and said their final good-byes to the dog that had meant so much to Randy.

That night as they were getting ready for bed, Randy's parents were sharing their heartache with each other when Barbara said, "John . . . shhh. Do you hear something?"

"It sounds like scratching," he answered. "It can't be the girls' cats. They're both in the girls' room."

"It's coming from the back door," she said. "Like the sound Bingo used to make when he scratched the door to be let in."

John ran into the kitchen and flung open the back door. He looked around with a crazy ray of hope that Bingo somehow would be standing outside, waiting to be let in. But of course the dog wasn't there.

Meanwhile, in the girls' room, the cats began pacing the floor, mewing and meowing with their tails fluffed up out of fear.

"What's bugging them?" asked Suzy.

"Maybe it's something outside," Debbie replied. She opened the window and then shouted for her sister. "Suzy! Come here quick! What do you hear outside?"

There was no doubt about it. Both girls could plainly hear a distinctive bark—a cross between an old man's cough and a hoarse coyote. Mixed in with the barks were whimpers, whines, and howls. "That's Bingo!" Suzy cried out. "I can tell his bark anywhere!"

Debbie burst out of the room and almost ran into her parents in the hallway. "Mom! Dad! Bingo's alive! We can hear him barking!"

"It can't be," Barbara said as she and John raced to the window and peered outside. They also clearly heard Bingo's bark. "It's coming from the backyard near the elm tree!"

"That's where we buried Bingo," said John. "Maybe he really is alive! Maybe we buried him by mistake—maybe he was just in a coma!"

John dashed out of the room. But the moment he bolted outside, the barking ceased. Still, John sprinted to the freshly dug grave to see if somehow the dog had clawed his way out. But the grave had not been disturbed.

"Girls," said John, "we have to face facts. Bingo is dead. What we heard must have been another dog that sounds very much like Bingo."

"We know every dog in this neighborhood," said Suzy. "We know every dog in this *town*. There aren't any dogs that sound like Bingo."

"Well, maybe it's a stray. Who knows? Come on, let's all get some sleep."

The next night, the same barking—accompanied by the mournful whining and howling—continued to haunt the entire family again, keeping them up for much of the night. Determined to find the source of the barking, John searched the entire area. But he found nothing. "Whenever I went to one part of the yard, the barking seemed to come from the other side," he told Barbara. "Sometimes it didn't seem to come from anywhere, and yet it seemed to come from everywhere."

The sorrowful barking tore at the hearts of the Stevens family. The girls cried, the parents fretted, and even the cats yowled.

"John," said Barbara, "what if it really is Bingo?"

"You know it can't be him."

"But what if the barking is from Bingo's ghost?"

"Bingo's ghost?" he exclaimed, throwing his hands up in the air. "Have you flipped your lid?"

"No, I haven't. I think it is Bingo's ghost and that he'll keep barking until we bury him where he should be buried—next to Randy's grave. Since Bingo and Randy were so close in life, why shouldn't they remain close in death?"

"But the cemetery director said—"

"John, how about doing what Randy and Bingo would have wanted."

He thought a moment and nodded. "You know, you're absolutely right."

John and Barbara dug up Bingo's grave, put the dog's wrapped body in the trunk of the car, and drove to the cemetery in the middle of the night. John neatly dug a hole next to his son's tombstone, making sure to remove the sod carefully. "I hope we don't get caught," John whispered. "They'll think we're grave robbers or something."

"Or really nuts," added Barbara.

Once Bingo was placed in the hole, they replaced the sod so that no one would notice the area had been disturbed. Then they stepped back and bowed their heads. "Bingo," said Barbara, "you're with Randy now. You two are together again— forever."

As they walked away, John and Barbara stopped in their tracks. They heard barking, but not the sad wailing from the previous two nights. No, this was happy, joyous barking—just like Bingo made whenever he played with his beloved friend, Randy Stevens.

* * *

"So, Aunt Suzy," asked Alex, "the cemetery people still don't know?"

"No, they never found out. It's remained a family secret— Bingo's secret." She patted the ground beside Randy's grave. "Ever since the night that Bingo was buried here, we've been comforted by knowing that they're with each other."

"Did the barking stop at your house?" Alex asked.

"Yes. However, over the years, people have claimed that while walking by the cemetery late at night, they heard a little boy laugh and a dog bark."

THE HAUNTING VENGEANCE

January 4, 1949

Those eyes! Those blazing red eyes erupted in a fury so frightening that I couldn't breath. I couldn't even twitch. I desperately wanted to shut my eyes, to blot out the vengeful stare that burned into me.

But I was helpless, paralyzed by fear. I could do nothing but lay in bed and gaze out my window in disbelief at the ghostly eyes of the very same wolf I had killed one week ago.

* * *

The creepy words in the mysterious journal left 13-year-old Troy Bradford feeling a little skittish.

Troy and his father Jack were spending a weekend at a weather-beaten farmhouse in Manitoba, Canada, that had been in the Bradford family for years. It originally belonged to Troy's great uncle, Scully Bradford, an eccentric loner who got along better with his farm animals than he did with people.

Although he didn't see much of his family, Scully often wrote to his nieces and nephews on the holidays. He kept them informed of the rewards and hardships of operating a small farm—and sometimes told them stories about his favorite dairy cows, goats, chickens, and sheep. After his death in 1985 at the age of 77, the Bradfords decided to lease the farmland but keep Scully's farmhouse as a retreat for the family.

Troy and his dad were staying the weekend to make a few simple repairs to the place. After putting in new weather stripping around the windows and doors, they began tackling the next project—re-cementing several rocks that had come loose in the stone fireplace.

While Jack was outside mixing the cement, Troy was jiggling each stone to see which ones needed to be secured. During his task, he pulled out a softball-sized rock from the fireplace and thought, *That's funny. This stone has never had any cement on it.* He peeked in the hole where the rock had been and discovered a small brown book hidden inside. *I wonder what that is?*

Troy reached in and retrieved an old journal bound in cracked and peeling leather. He opened it to the first page where the title "Renegade" was scrawled in black pen. The rest of the book was handwritten in bold, flowery strokes on delicate paper yellowed with age.

Troy carefully thumbed to a page at random. That's when he came upon the entry from January 4, 1949—the passage about the fiery red eyes of a ghost wolf.

"Dad!" shouted Troy. "Come here and look what I found!"

Jack examined the journal and said, "Why, this is from Uncle Scully. I recognize his handwriting. He used to send me the most interesting letters when I was a kid."

"Who's Renegade?"

"That name sounds familiar, but I can't quite place it. Let's read the first entry and see what it says."

March 14, 1948

I have decided to keep a diary about my newest four-legged friend. He is an abandoned baby wolf, about a month old, that I found in the hollow of a log. I looked around for signs of his mother and siblings, but found none. There are usually a half dozen cubs in each litter. It's obvious that this cub has been deprived of the warmth and tenderness of a family and has not suckled on mother's milk for some time. He was shivering and wet, and my heart would not allow nature to take its course and let him die. I have adopted this little wolf pup. I shall call him Renegade.

My fellow farmers will not be pleased with my actions, for wolves are the enemies of farmers. I am fully aware that these creatures hunt alone or in pairs in the summer and prey upon farmers' chickens, piglets, and sheep. Is it no wonder that these canines are despised and hated!

Yet I feel for this tiny wolf. I can no more slay it or let it die than I could take the life of my prize sheep, Melody. I believe there is good in all wild animals, even the wolf. It is resourceful, intelligent, and cunning. And I, for one, intend to prove that with patience and love, the wolf can be raised to serve as man's good, if not best, friend.

"Now, I remember!" Jack told Troy. "Renegade was the wolf Uncle Scully raised from infancy. He wrote to me about him once when the wolf was growing up. I seem to recall that Renegade died when he was about a year old. It's strange, but Uncle Scully never mentioned him again."

Every few days in the journal, Scully detailed the progress he made caring for the cub, nurturing him, gaining his trust, and training him. By the end of summer, Renegade had learned to sit, heel, retrieve things, come when called, and leave the farm animals alone.

September 8, 1948

Everybody tells me that the only good wolf is a dead wolf. My fellow farmers and stockmen have declared war on these fierce proud animals. So far this year, more than 100 wolves have been shot in the township, and most everyone is determined to wipe all wolves off the face of the earth.

How wrong they are! These animals must be protected.

Renegade is proof. He has grown into a handsome specimen. His sleek body quivers with strong muscles under a rich coat of spun silver. A wide bronze-colored ring around his neck reminds me of an Egyptian king's necklace.

He is, by his very nature, unique. Unlike his fellow wolves in this region, he is gifted with a mark that is solely his—an extra sixth toe on both his front feet and only three toes, one less than normal, on each hind foot.

I am spellbound by his eyes, which radiate an intelligence beyond my own understanding. They are wise eyes, yet wild and sly enough to make me feel the slightest bit fearful. I know his blood flows with centuries of a killer's instinct. Yet I see in him a kindness and an acceptance that we share a common bond of trust.

October 25, 1948

   People no longer make fun of me. Now they consider me crazy because twice this week I have ordered hunters off my land for trying to shoot my wolf. They accuse me of harboring a fugitive, a member of a family of murderers. But this is guilt by association, for Renegade is no killer.

   Yes, I lost a calf and a goat over the summer to wolves. But Renegade was not involved. I saw the proof in the mud. The pawprints of the predators were not Renegade's. He is not wild. He is my pet, and I have tamed him.

November 23, 1948

   My animals haven't been bothered with any wolf attacks since early summer. I'm beginning to wonder if Renegade has told his fellow wolves to keep out because this is his territory. He is my farm's guardian. I feel he's watching over me and my animals, not preying on us. When I hear him howl at night, it soothes me, for it is not a wailing cry but a bay of contentment.

December 28, 1948

   What have I done? How could I have made such a horrible blunder? My heart is crushed under the weight of enormous regret. But there is nothing I can do to alter the tragic events of this awful day.

   I had just returned home from gathering supplies in town when I heard the terrified bleating of my prize-winning sheep, Melody. She was so beautiful. She had won the blue ribbon for best of show at the fair last year. When I raced to the corral, Melody lie dying. She had been brutally mauled. And standing over her was none other than my so-called friend, Renegade, with blood dripping from his fangs.

I had been betrayed! Once a wolf, always a wolf! How could I have been so stupid! How absurd of me to believe that my love and patience held power over the ways of nature and the instincts of the wild.

My precious lamb took her final breaths. And what of this vicious traitor of a wolf who had taken her life? He stood defiantly, staring at me as if he were mocking me for trusting him.

The anger that swelled up inside me erupted like a volcano. In one fell swoop, I reached for my rifle and shot Renegade. I leaped high in the air in victory, for he died instantly. My joy and rage knew no bounds. I had slain the killer!

My emotions were short-lived, however. They withered the moment I discovered the horrifying truth. When I reached the lifeless wolf and my fatally wounded sheep, I stopped dead in my tracks.

On the ground, on the other side of the water trough that had blocked my view from the back porch, lay the body of an enormous gray wolf with its throat torn. I stood still, not understanding at first what had occurred.

I stared long and hard at the paw prints in the mud until the truth hit me like a thunderbolt.

Renegade had not attacked Melody! No, the other wolf had committed the deed. Renegade, my trusted friend, had come to my sheep's rescue! He had defended her by fighting the lone wolf to the death. The blood on Renegade's fangs was not from Melody but from the other wolf!

If only I had known. If only I had believed in him. Now Renegade is dead by my own hand!

I am too heartsick to write anymore tonight.

"So that's why Uncle Scully never wrote anything more about Renegade in his letters to me," Jack told Troy. "He was too upset and hurt. If word got out that he mistakenly shot his pet wolf, people would have made even more fun of him. He simply told me and everyone else that Renegade died. Uncle Scully never gave us any explanation."

"He hid the journal so no one would know," added Troy.

"Why didn't he simply destroy the journal?" Jack wondered. "Why did he keep it?"

"Dad, Uncle Scully wrote some spooky stuff after Renegade died. When I first found the journal, I thumbed through it and read a page that gave me the shivers."

With his dad looking over his shoulder, Troy reread the beginning of that entry, which continued beyond what he had read earlier.

January 4, 1949

Those eyes! Those blazing red eyes erupted in a fury so frightening that I couldn't breathe. I couldn't even twitch. I desperately wanted to shut my eyes, to blot out the vengeful stare that burned into me.

But I was helpless, paralyzed by fear. I could do nothing but lie in bed and gaze out my window in disbelief at the ghostly eyes of the very same wolf I had killed one week ago.

There can be no doubt it was Renegade, even though I did not see his whole body. I saw only those unblinking glaring eyes framed in a faint image of a wolf's face that floated eerily above the ground.

Earlier that night I had gone to sleep, bundled up in my favorite quilt as the temperature plunged to the coldest of the new winter season.

At some point in the darkest of the night, the ghost appeared. I do not know how long he hovered outside my window, but eventually the intensity of his stare interrupted my slumber, and I awoke in a paralyzing terror.

I lost all sense of time. For minutes, maybe for hours, our eyes remained locked on each other, and I felt forced to relive over and over again that ghastly moment when I killed Renegade.

Finally, the wolf's eyes faded into the blackness, and my breathing become as labored as if I had sprinted the breadth and width of my entire farm.

Try as I might, I could not escape this appalling conclusion: Renegade has returned from the dead to haunt me.

"Wow!" shouted Troy. "That's incredible! Do you think Uncle Scully really saw Renegade's ghost?"

"Only in his mind, Troy. If anything, the haunting was a dream. Or a figment of his imagination."

"Let's read on."

January 22, 1949

Those haunting eyes of hatred returned again! Only this time they were not outside my window. They were floating above the foot of my bed!

As before, I was roused from a deep sleep only to be frozen from fright by hateful eyes that glowed like embers. To torment me further, Renegade's ghost bared his deadly razor-sharp fangs, causing my terror to build unmercifully. Then he gave a menacing snarl that came from the very depths of all that is vile and wicked.

He seemed to be ready to pounce, to sink his murderous teeth into me. But even though I felt my life was about to end in a painful death, I could not move a muscle nor scream in panic, so profound was my fear. Still, those glowering eyes and lethal fangs moved not one inch closer to me. The savage snarl did not grow any louder.

When I could stand it no more, I shrieked in my mind, "Go ahead! Get it over with! Kill me, Renegade, kill me!"

And in an instant, everything was dark and quiet. For a crazed moment, I wondered if I was dead. But when I gathered my wits, I looked out the window and saw the moon beaming its soft light over the snow-swept prairie. I could feel the chill of my exhausted, sweat-soaked body. I felt no pain, only the aches of untold stress and anxiety.

I was still alive and now free of the ghost.

And then I heard a distant, fiendish howling that curdled my blood. It was the baying of a cold, ruthless brute. It was the ghost of Renegade. I knew then that he would be back again. I just did not know when.

According to Uncle Scully's journal, Renegade's ghost continued to haunt him on two or three occasions a year, at different times, on different nights.

"Dad, look at the dates. He was haunted from 1949 . . ." Troy flipped to the last entry in the book ". . . up until 1985."

"That was the year Uncle Scully died. I had no idea he was tormented for the rest of his life."

"Now do you believe in Renegade's ghost?"

"No, Troy. I don't think there ever was a ghost. It was all in his mind. Uncle Scully was racked with such guilt that he imagined all these hauntings. There's no such thing as a ghost— especially of a wolf. Besides, people in the family have spent time out here since Uncle Scully's death, and no one has ever mentioned seeing or hearing anything unusual.

"Keep in mind that Uncle Scully loved writing. I believe that every time he got pangs of guilt, he jotted down a description of an imaginary haunting. Poor Uncle Scully, his conscience never let him forget that he killed Renegade."

Sunday evening, long after it had turned dark, Troy and his father finished their work, closed up the house, and hopped into the car. They turned off the farm road onto the highway when Troy shouted, "Hey, Dad, look over by the shoulder. Is that a wolf?"

About 30 yards (27 m) ahead of them, their headlights shined on a silver-colored wolf trotting in the same direction as they were. Suddenly, the wolf turned around and sprang to the center of the highway directly in front of the moving car.

"Look out, Dad! You're going to hit him!"

Jack hit the brakes and jerked the steering wheel hard to the left as the car skidded to a stop off the road. "Oh, no!" cried Troy. "We hit him!"

Jack grabbed a flashlight out of the trunk. He and Troy ran back to the spot where they thought they had run over the wolf. But after searching the pavement for several minutes, Jack said, "I guess we missed him."

"We had to have hit him," said Troy. "We both saw him leap in front of us and then stand there as we drove right over him."

Jack checked the front end of the car, looking for signs that he had struck the wolf. "There is no blood, dent, or strands of fur on the fender. Somehow, some way, we missed him."

Suddenly, a howl shattered the nighttime quiet. "Dad! Behind you!"

Jack wheeled around, and his flashlight beamed at the profile of a wolf howling on the shoulder across the highway. The sleek animal had a coat seemingly made of spun silver, a bronze-colored ring of fur around his neck, and a thick, black tail.

The wolf stopped howling and then slowly turned its face and stared, with glowing red eyes, directly at Troy and his father.

"His eyes, Dad! They look like they're on fire!"

"Yes, I see. And something else is very odd. There's no shadow behind him. The light seems to be going right through him!"

The wolf turned his head away from them and continued his baying. Then he slowly faded away.

Troy and his father hurried to the spot where the wolf had disappeared. They found nothing of the wolf except the footprints he left behind in the soft dirt.

"Look at the paw prints!" exclaimed Troy. "Six toes and three toes! Dad, we just saw the ghost of Renegade!"

THE GHOST OF WALKER'S BAY

I'm drowning! I'm drowning!

As she slipped under the water, Chelsea Emerson began to panic. *I don't want to die!*

Moments earlier, the nine-year-old girl had been taking a sunrise stroll on the deck of her parents' 40-foot (12-m) sailboat, the *Sea Ya*. It was anchored in Walker's Bay, a quarter mile (.4 km) offshore of a small island in the Bahamas. Because she could barely swim, Chelsea was supposed to wear her life jacket whenever she was topside. But, having just awakened, the sleepy girl in her oversized T-shirt carried the vest in her hand rather than putting it on.

Up on deck at the back of the yacht, Chelsea was watching the flight of a squadron of pelicans and not paying attention to where she was walking. She tripped over a coiled-up rope and pitched forward. Her head smacked into the railing that encircled the deck and nearly knocked her out. Dazed and confused, Chelsea dropped her life jacket, staggered a few feet, and then tumbled over the railing and into the blue-green Caribbean.

Unable to come to her senses, Chelsea slid under the sea. Finally, as water rushed into her nose, she recovered enough for her survival instincts to take over. She flailed her arms wildly, trying desperately to reach the surface. *Get to the top!* she told herself. *You need air now or you're going to die! Kick, Chelsea, kick!* She burst through the surface and gulped the air. But before she could yell for help, she went under again.

As she fought to stay afloat, panic set in and Chelsea forgot everything she had learned about water safety. She didn't remain calm . . . she didn't remember to lean back and hold her breath so she could naturally float to the surface. All Chelsea knew was that she was underwater and facing death.

By now, Chelsea began to feel her strength seeping from her body. She knew she didn't have much time left before she lost her battle with the sea. With one last effort, she clawed her way to the surface and uttered a weak cry for help—one that her sleeping parents below deck couldn't hear.

With no one on the remote beach to help her, Chelsea knew she was doomed. Slipping again under the sea, she held her breath until her lungs felt as if they were on fire. *I can't hold out any longer. It's all over. I'm going to die.* She was ready to give in to the urge to stop struggling.

Suddenly, out of nowhere, she was yanked by the top

of her T-shirt and pulled to the surface. Gagging, sputtering, and coughing, Chelsea gulped life-giving air into her burning lungs. *Oh, thank goodness, someone has saved me!* Totally exhausted and too weak to utter anything but, "Don't let go of me," Chelsea turned around to see who had rescued her—and couldn't believe her eyes.

It wasn't a person—it was a tan and black German shepherd! The dog released its grip on her T-shirt, and Chelsea frantically clutched its right hind leg. The worn-out girl barely had enough strength left to hold on. Using powerful paddling strokes, the dog slowly and steadily made its way toward shore, towing Chelsea to safety.

When they finally reached the shallow water, Chelsea let go, staggered onto the beach, crumpled in a heap, and passed out. She awoke after the German shepherd began licking her face.

Chelsea threw her arms around the dog's neck. "Oh, thank you, thank you, thank you," she said. "You saved my life." The dog wagged its tail and backed away. Then it looked toward the *Sea Ya* and began barking loudly and madly.

Still trying to catch her breath, Chelsea remained sprawled on her back on the sand. When the barking stopped, she sat up only to discover that the dog was gone. She glanced in all directions, but there was no sign of the lifesaving German shepherd.

Meanwhile, back on the sailboat, Chelsea's parents, Ken and Ellen, had awakened and noticed that their daughter wasn't in her berth. When they didn't find her topside, they started shouting, "Chelsea! Chelsea! Where are you?"

"Oh, no!" Ken cried out. "I've found her life jacket here at the stern!"

"Please don't tell me she fell overboard!" Ellen screamed. They frantically scanned the water, yelling, "Chelsea! Chelsea!"

On the beach, Chelsea heard her parents' desperate shouts for her. She waved to them and hollered back, "Over here! Over here!"

"There she is!" cried Ellen with joyous relief. "On the beach! Oh, thank goodness, she's alive!"

Ken and Ellen hopped into their dinghy and quickly rowed to shore, where they hugged and kissed their frightened, weary daughter.

"Chelsea, what happened?" asked her father. "Are you all right?"

Chelsea broke down and cried. "I fell overboard . . ." she said between sobs ". . . and I was drowning . . . and I thought I was going to die . . . and then this big dog rescued me." She cried even harder and longer. When she finally regained her composure, she gave a detailed account of her rescue.

"That's an amazing story, sweetheart," said Ellen. Chelsea then caught her mother and father glancing at each other in a way that indicated they doubted her account.

"You *do* believe me, don't you?" Chelsea asked.

"All that matters is that you're safe," said Ken.

"Did you see the dog?" asked the little girl. "Did you hear her barking?"

"No, darling, we didn't," Ellen replied.

"She was a big German shepherd," said Chelsea. "Tan-colored with dark brown spots. I wonder where she went."

"Let's get you back to the boat," said her mother.

Later that morning, while Chelsea was resting below deck, she overheard her parents talking about her ordeal.

"What do you think really happened, Ken?"

"I don't think a dog rescued her, that's for sure," he said. "There aren't any other boats anchored in this bay. The beach is pretty remote, although there is a village on the other side of the island. Besides, I didn't see any paw prints in the sand."

"They could have been washed away by the waves."

"But only if the dog walked along the edge of the water. The beach is very long and empty, and we would have seen the dog—unless it swam out into the water. And no dog is going to do that."

"If there wasn't a dog, then who saved her?"

"I think Chelsea was in such a state of panic and confusion that her mind played tricks on her. More than likely, she made it to shore on her own and simply imagined the dog."

Chelsea had heard enough. She stormed up to the deck and declared, "I don't care what you think. I know what happened to me. A German shepherd saved my life!"

* * *

About a half mile (.8 km) away, at the other end of Walker's Bay, 12-year-old Rachel Katz stepped out of her family's rented beach house, carrying her flippers, mask, and snorkel. With only one day left of their vacation before the Katz family had to return home to New York, Rachel was determined to get in as much water time as possible.

While the rest of her family was eating breakfast, Rachel, a superb swimmer, stepped into the gentle warm surf and began snorkeling toward a coral reef about 75 yards (69 m) from shore. Rachel floated on her stomach and watched below as a starfish wrapped its five 6-inch- (15-cm-) long arms over a clamshell. The girl took a deep breath and headed down for a closer look. As she hovered over the starfish, she saw a shadow move across the ocean bottom. Her first thought was, *Oh my gosh, it's a shark—and it's swimming between me and the surface!* She fearfully gazed up and then blinked. *Hey, that's no shark. That's a dog!*

Rachel rose to the surface and pulled off her mask to get a better look. About 30 yards (27 m) away from her, a tan German shepherd with dark brown spots was paddling at a fast clip out toward the open water.

Rachel started to swim after the dog, but she had promised her parents that she wouldn't go out past the reef. So she climbed onto a rock that stuck out of the surf.

Where is that dog going? she wondered. Shading her eyes from the rising sun, Rachel scanned the horizon. She saw no other snorkeler, scuba diver, or swimmer. There wasn't another boat in sight except for a yacht on the other side of the curved bay. She noticed that two adults from the sailboat had jumped into a dinghy and were rowing to shore where a lone figure—a young girl—was waving to them. Judging from their actions, Rachel figured there was no connection between them and the dog.

Rachel whistled. "Hey, dog, come back here!" She whistled again, but the dog didn't slow down or change its course. The German shepherd kept paddling out to sea.

Suddenly, the dog barked three times—like the happy barks a dog gives when he sees his master come home—and then disappeared under the water.

What happened to the dog? Where is she? Oh, no! She better come back up. Rachel waited for the dog to reappear. One minute, two minutes, three minutes went by and still no dog.

"Oh, my gosh," she said out loud. "She's drowned! This is terrible!"

Rachel jumped off the rock, swam back to shore, and dashed to the house. "Mom! Dad! I saw a big dog—it was a German shepherd—swimming in the ocean. Then she just disappeared under the water. I waited and waited, but she never surfaced. I'm afraid she's in trouble—or probably drowned. Can we go look for her?"

"Let's use the jet ski," said her father.

Moments later, Rachel and her dad were out on the water, crisscrossing back and forth around the spot where the dog was last seen. But there was no sign of the German shepherd anywhere.

As they returned to the beach, Rachel wondered out loud, "Why would a dog swim out to sea?"

* * *

That evening, the townspeople on the other side of the

island threw a beach party in honor of their village's birthday. Over open fires, cooks were preparing conch fritters and fish kabobs. A steel-drum band filled the air with reggae music, and people of all ages were doing the limbo.

At the party, Chelsea and Rachel met for the first time when the older girl was getting her black hair tightly braided by a Bahamian woman.

"Oh, that corn-rowed hair looks so pretty," Chelsea told Rachel. "Especially the braids with the colorful beads."

"Thanks," said Rachel. "It's my last night in the Bahamas, and I wanted to do something outrageous."

The two girls struck up a conversation and began talking about the fun they had on their vacations.

As Chelsea told her new friend about the various islands she had visited, Rachel's eyes locked on a German shepherd—tan with brown spots—that was walking briskly through the crowd.

Could that be the dog I saw in the ocean today? Rachel wondered. *It sure looks like her. I hope it is. Then I'll feel better, knowing she's all right. I need to get a closer look at her.*

"Excuse me, Chelsea," said Rachel, "but there's a dog over there that I want to catch."

Chelsea followed Rachel's eyes and saw the German shepherd. "That's her! That's the dog!"

"You know that dog?"

"It's a long story, but she saved my life this morning! Let's go!"

The girls ran into the crowd and followed the dog until she turned up a side street. The dog stopped at a bright green wooden house with red trim and blue shutters. The dog hopped onto the front porch and lay down.

The girls approached the dog carefully. She wagged her tail and let them pet her. "I wonder," said Chelsea. "It could be the same dog, but I'm not sure."

"What are you talking about?"

Chelsea told Rachel about how she had fallen off the sailboat and was drowning before the German shepherd rescued her and pulled her to shore. "Then the dog disappeared."

"That's incredible!" Rachel exclaimed. "I saw that same tan and brown dog right afterwards. She was heading out to sea. Then she barked and went under the water, and I never saw her again. Until now, maybe." Rachel studied the German shepherd. "She looks smaller and darker than the one I saw."

The girls jumped when the door to the house opened unexpectedly. The dog sprang to her feet and barked warmly. A large Bahamian woman in a pink straw hat and matching flowered dress stepped onto the porch.

"Well, hello there young ladies." Turning to the dog, the woman said, "Miss Molly, did you bring these lovely lasses over to our house?"

"Uh, well, sort of," said Chelsea. "We kind of followed her. You see, she looks like the dog that saved my life this morning. I fell overboard, and a German shepherd came out of nowhere and pulled me to shore."

Rachel piped in, "And I was wondering if this is the

same dog I saw swimming out to sea this morning. She just vanished, and I was afraid she drowned. I was hoping your dog was the one I saw and that she's okay."

"Really?" said the woman, her eyes wide open. "Now this is amazing. This is really amazing." Pointing to two wicker rockers on the front porch, she told the girls, "Come sit a spell. I might have an answer for you both—but you may not believe it."

She sat down with a grunt, her wooden rocking chair making a creaking sound from her ample weight. "First things first. My name is Janelle. What's yours?"

"Chelsea Emerson."

"Rachel Katz."

"So, Chelsea, you were saved from drowning by a German shepherd and, Rachel, you saw the same dog swimming out to sea?" Janelle quickened the pace of her rocking chair. "This could be the day. Yes, indeed. After all these years, she could finally be free."

"What are you talking about?" asked Rachel.

"Now, girls, I don't want to disappoint you, but Miss Molly here is not the dog you saw today. Miss Molly is probably the only German shepherd in the world who hates the water. And here she is living on a tiny island surrounded by the sea."

Janelle stopped rocking and scooted her chair closer to the girls. In a hushed tone, she announced, "What you saw, I'm pretty sure, was Sheba—Sheba the ghost."

"Ghost?" both girls squealed at the same time.

"May my hair turn from black to blonde if I'm lying. Yes, on the far side of the island, Sheba has been seen in the water and on the beach since way back in the late 1800s. Want to hear about it?"

The girls nodded eagerly.

"There was this sailing ship, the *Richmond*, that was traveling from Cuba to Bermuda. About 20 people were on board, including the Winchester family—two grade-school girls named Nancy and Polly and their parents. They also had a dog with them, a German shepherd named Sheba. Their father was in the exporting business and was moving the family to Bermuda.

"They set sail on a pretty day. The fore-topsail was run up, and they glided along with the gentle tide on a southern breeze. Unknown to the crew and passengers, a hurricane was already in full force less than 500 miles (805 km) away. It was bearing down rapidly on the Bahama Channel. Two days out from Cuba, the seas began churning, and the skies took on the threatening color of an impending storm. There's an old seamen's saying: 'Red skies in the morning, sailors take warning. Red skies at night, sailors' delight.' Well, it was a red sky that morning.

"Before the passengers on the *Richmond* knew it, the hurricane struck. It was ferocious. The winds howled. The waves turned into the hands of an angry monster, smashing and tossing the ship willy-nilly.

"The Winchesters and their dog huddled below deck, wondering if the next wave would pitch the ship on its side. Above them, they heard the sickening sound of the masts cracking, splitting, and toppling. The sails soon collapsed, and the ship was completely at the mercy of the tempest.

"Hour after hour, the *Richmond* was battered and shoved helplessly toward the shallows and the deadly reefs off this island. Mr. Winchester used rope to tie the girls to separate pieces of wood so that if they were pitched into the sea they might float. But before he could finish, the waves slammed the ship against the reef, cracking it open like a coconut. The splintered hull of the wooden ship spilled its cargo and its passengers into the sea.

"Nancy and Polly held onto Sheba as they tumbled into the water. But the furious waves ripped the dog from their arms. Sheba looked around at the broken pieces of the ship and found Nancy clinging to a board and crying for help. She was slipping and about to give up.

"Sheba paddled over to the girl, who grabbed a hold of the dog's hind leg. Then Sheba towed her safely to the shore where Nancy collapsed from exhaustion."

"That's exactly how the dog saved me today!" Chelsea declared.

"Yes indeed," said Janelle. "And that's very important to this story. Now where was I? Oh, yes, Sheba was dog tired—no pun intended—but her ears perked up. She heard the faint cry of another child."

"Was it Polly?" asked Rachel.

"Yes. Little Polly was hanging for dear life on the broken mast that was floating in the water. But the current was pushing her out to sea. Sheba swam back out, even though she was exhausted after battling the waves and rescuing Nancy. That dog loved both those girls so much.

"Nancy waited and waited on the beach, yearning to be reunited with her sister and their faithful dog Sheba. But, alas, it was not meant to be. Neither Sheba nor Polly was ever seen again."

Rachel shook her head. "Oh, how sad!"

"Yes, such a terrible tragedy. Poor Nancy was overcome with grief. She lost her parents and her sister—and her dog. The bodies of the other passengers eventually washed ashore. But they never found the bodies of Polly Winchester or Sheba."

"But what does this have to do with us?" asked Chelsea.

"Perhaps more than you could ever imagine. You see, girls, ever since that deadly hurricane, a strange sight has appeared every few years in Walker's Bay. Someone—it could be a fisherman, a tourist, a shell hunter—will see a tan and brown German shepherd swim out to sea and simply disappear under the water."

"Sheba's ghost?" asked Rachel.

"Yes, Sheba's ghost. Some of us on the island believe that Sheba has been a tormented spirit, searching in vain for little Polly. It tugs at your heart, doesn't it? To think that the power of love between a dog and a girl could be so strong."

"This is going to sound stupid, but do you think that Sheba saved my life?" asked Chelsea.

"*Think?* I am totally, absolutely, positively convinced that's exactly what happened to you."

"You said earlier that 'this could be the day' and that 'she could finally be free,'" Rachel recalled. "What did you mean?"

"I believe that ghosts have some unfinished business," explained Janelle. "In this case, Sheba couldn't rest because she died before saving Polly. Sheba's spirit had been roaming the waters here for nearly a century, waiting to finish her task. Then Chelsea showed up. When she fell overboard and was drowning, Sheba was there to save her life—the life of a young girl. Sheba's spirit no longer needs to wander the waters. She's now free to go wherever spirits are supposed to go."

"But I saw the dog too," said Rachel. "And that was after Chelsea was rescued."

"I believe that what you saw was Sheba finally being free from the torment of the last 100 years. May I ask you a question? Did she bark before she disappeared?"

"Yes she did," Rachel replied.

"She was saying good-bye to this world," explained Janelle. "No one in this life will ever see her again. She's at peace now."

THE PHANTOM CAT

It was love at first sight.

Seven-year-old Tara Owens had gone to the hairdresser's with her mother, Clarice. They learned from the stylist that a cute, helpless kitten had been abandoned at the front door of the beauty shop earlier that morning. "He's in the back room," the stylist told Tara.

Before Clarice could say a word, Tara scampered into the back room where a tiny furball of gray and black stripes was curled up on the floor on a crunched-up sheet.

"Oh, aren't you just so sweet!" Tara squealed, picking up the sleepy kitten. "And look, your paws are all white!" Cradling the cat in her arms, Tara took a deep breath and walked out into the main room.

Her mother eyed her suspiciously and warned, "Now I don't want you begging me about keeping that cat. We already have a dog."

"But Sampson is Donnell's dog. If my brother can have a pet, I should be able to have one too."

"I don't know," her mom said warily.

"Mama! Pleeeeease. I promise I'll take care of him. I'll feed him every morning and at night, and I'll brush him and I'll love him. *Pleeeeease?*"

"Your daddy isn't fond of cats. I don't think he'll go for it."

Tara rushed up to Clarice and gave her a big kiss. "Oh, thank you, Mama."

"I didn't say you can keep him."

"I saw the way you looked at him. You like him already. Isn't he the cutest thing? Look at his white paws. I've already got a name picked out for him—Sneakers."

When they got home, Tara's father, Clarence, took one look at the mewing kitten and said, "No way!"

"But, Daddy, you always taught me to help others in need. Well, this kitty is homeless. And we've got a home." Clarence shook his head. He knew he was licked. And that's how Sneakers became a part of the Owens household.

* * *

Sneakers was no ordinary cat. A mixed breed of equal parts mischief and smarts, he had the family giggling at him one moment and scolding him the next. But he was always lovable.

The cat showed his intelligence when he was just six months old. One of the first things Tara bought Sneakers was a wooden brush with soft plastic bristles. The cat loved it when she groomed him. He arched his back and purred and then flipped over on his belly to make sure Tara brushed his entire coat.

He often spent his daytime naps lying in front of the floor vent in the downstairs bathroom where he could keep warm in the winter and cool in the summer. Because that's where Tara usually brushed him, she always left the brush on the floor by the wall next to the vent.

One day while Tara was watching television, she heard a banging noise coming from the downstairs bathroom. Her mother was upstairs, and no one else was in the house. Tara discovered that Sneakers was picking up the bristles of the brush with his teeth, raising his head high, and then throwing the brush down on the floor. He stopped only when he saw that Tara was watching him.

From then on, Sneakers whacked the brush on the bathroom floor whenever he wanted more food, water, treats, or grooming. Sometimes he did it as a reminder to Tara that his litter box needed changing.

Sneakers loved to hide—especially in large paper shopping bags from the department store where Tara's mother worked. Whenever he saw an empty bag, his eyes widened in happy anticipation of playing in a new hiding spot. Clarice would place the bag on its side and walk away. Sneakers then would stick his head in the bag before jumping inside and rolling around.

One time, Clarice left an empty shopping bag at the top of the stairs. Sneakers immediately dove into the bag and began scratching the sides and thoroughly enjoying his paper hideaway. Meanwhile, Tara was talking on the phone in her bedroom when she heard a muffled yowl, followed by a series of soft thuds. When she went to investigate, Tara found the paper bag at the bottom of the stairs and Sneakers staring at it with angry eyes and bent-back ears.

Sneakers displayed bad eating manners. At the dinner table, he would sit patiently by Tara's feet. Then after watching his owner take a bite or two, he would spring onto her lap, study her plate, and decide what to taste. In the blink of an eye, his paw would swipe at a French fry or pea or kernel of corn and knock it to the floor. Next, he would swiftly leap to the floor and bat the food around before gulping it down like one of the moths he occasionally chased and caught.

Sneakers couldn't help himself when it came to drinks, either. He had to sample whatever Tara was having. He'd jump on her lap, dip his paw in her glass, and then lick off the drops. It didn't matter if she was having milk or root beer, he wanted a taste. Once satisfied, he'd go on his merry way, often leaving a trail of wet paw prints behind.

"That cat doesn't belong near the dinner table," Clarence would growl. "And, Tara, don't you go feeding him any table scraps either." But everyone—including Clarence—knew she secretly did anyway.

Her father and Sneakers never quite hit it off. Clarence wasn't a cat person—and Sneakers knew it. Their relationship remained a stormy one because of the way the cat loved to irritate him.

Whenever Tara's father worked late at the accounting firm, he came home and usually threw his clothes on the bedroom chair and draped his necktie over the door handle of the closet.

Sneakers quickly turned his tie into a hanging piece of exercise equipment. The cat would sneak into the bedroom and jump up and knock the tie to the floor. Then he'd bat it around and leave it in a crumpled—and sometimes shredded—mess under the bed.

The cat got along better with Sampson the dog, a likeable spaniel, than he did with Tara's father. The only time Sneakers would pester the dog was when Sampson slept on the floor where the sunlight beamed through the window on a cold winter's day. Sneakers would boldly walk over and swipe him across the snout, sending the dog yelping, more out of surprise than fear. Sneakers would then curl up on the very same spot the dog had just left.

One of Sneakers' great joys was waking up anyone who slept late, especially Tara's brother Donnell. Sneakers would march into his room, leap onto the end table, and start knocking everything off of it—Donnell's billfold, watch, pen, and any loose change—until Donnell woke up and yelled at the cat.

On the other hand, Sneakers, who slept on the bed with Tara, acted sweet and gentle when it came to waking up his mistress.

He would pounce on her pillow, which usually awakened her. But Tara would pretend she was sleeping. Sneakers then would walk so close to her that she could feel the tickle of his whiskers across her cheek. She would remain quiet, not opening her eyes. Sneakers would slip gently to the back of her head and nestle on her pillow and purr loudly. Then he would tap her head once or twice. Tara would smile, but still not move. Sneakers finally would pick up a strand of her hair with his needle-sharp teeth and tug hard. Tara would open her eyes real wide and shout, "Good morning!" The cat would leap backward as if he was totally shocked—which he wasn't, because they did this most every morning. Finally, he would hop onto her pillow and purr like a finely tuned engine.

For seven years, as the two grew up together, Sneakers proved to be a joy and a wonderful, loyal friend to Tara. He was always there for her. He sensed whenever Tara wasn't feeling well. Once, when Tara broke her ankle, she lay on her bed and cried, feeling sorry for herself. Sneakers hopped onto her bed, slipped his paws under her fingers, and rested his head on top of her hand. He stayed there for nearly an hour—a cat's way of holding his mistress' hand. The warmth Tara felt and the purring she heard helped soothe the pain.

He shared Tara's ups and downs. He brushed lovingly against her legs and purred happily whenever Tara came home waving the latest A on her math test. And he cuddled up next to her when she threw herself on the bed and cried after having a fight with her best friend Sandra.

No matter what was happening in Tara's life, she could always count on Sneakers to make her smile. She would pour out her heart and deepest secrets to her cat and always get a comforting warm purr in return.

As she neared her 15th birthday and her interest grew in boys, basketball, and choir, Tara spent less time at home. But no matter how busy she was, Tara still found a few minutes for a little one-on-one with her cat.

Maybe it was because she had less time with him; maybe it was because she hadn't been attentive enough. Whatever the reason, Tara didn't notice the slight physical changes in her cat. He wasn't eating well and wasn't as frisky as he once was.

She realized something was wrong when Sneakers failed to jump in her lap while she was munching on potato chips and drinking a soda. Sneakers seemed sluggish and in pain. Tara waited several days, hoping that he would get better, but he only got worse. She and her mother finally took him to veterinarian Dr. Karl Henning.

"I'm afraid I have bad news, Tara," Dr. Henning said, after examining the cat and running tests. "Your cat is suffering from a deadly disease called cystitis—tiny bits of gravel formed in the bladder that block the urinary tract. And he has a very bad heart."

Tara felt weak in the knees from the news and squeezed her mother's hand. "Can you fix him, doctor? Can you make him better?"

"I'm afraid not," the vet replied. "Surgery would be useless. It would just make him suffer more, and his chances of surviving the operation would be slim."

"I don't care!" Tara declared. "We must save him. He's my best friend."

"For now, the best thing we can do is nothing except keep him comfortable," said the vet. "Then in a month, we should discuss putting him to sleep."

"I won't do it, not to Sneakers!" Tara, frantic now, turned to her mother. "Mama, we can't put Sneakers to sleep! Please let's do the operation!"

"But it could kill him," argued her mother.

"It might save him too."

"It might keep him alive for only about six more months," explained the vet.

Clarice put her arm around her daughter's shoulder. "Do you really want Sneakers to suffer?"

"No, I want him to live—live as long as possible. He's my cat. I'll pay for the operation. I'll get a part-time job after school. Please!"

Her mother sighed and turned to the vet. "Well, Dr. Henning, can you perform the operation?"

"Yes, as long as you know the risks. He could die on the operating table. And the surgery won't cure him. It will extend his life for maybe half a year—if it's successful. There are no guarantees he'll make it. This could be his last night."

"No it won't," Tara declared. "Sneakers is not going to die." She held her cat tightly. "It *will* work. It *has* to work." She tenderly kissed him on his head. "I love you, Sneakers." He rubbed his cheek against her tear-soaked face.

* * *

Tara didn't sleep much that night, worrying about her beloved cat and the life-and-death operation he was facing. She tossed and turned and fretted. *Did I make the right decision? Oh, I hope so. What if he dies? He's not going to die. Am I being selfish? No, I want him to live as long as he can.*

The next morning, Tara did something she had never done before. She asked her mother if she could skip school. "I can't think of anything except Sneakers," she said.

Clarice understood. "Honey, under the circumstances, I think it'll be okay—but only this one time."

"Thanks, Mama. I'm going to take my bike and go down to the animal clinic. I want to be there in the waiting room while Dr. Henning operates."

When Tara arrived at the clinic, the vet had already

begun the surgery. Tara, her stomach tied up in knots, squirmed in her seat, hoping against hope that her cat would pull through the operation.

An hour later, Dr. Henning walked into the waiting room. Tara searched his face for a clue—a smile, a twinkle in his eye that everything was all right, that the operation was a success, that Sneakers would live for years and years. But there was no twinkle, no smile.

"Tara," he said, putting his hand on her trembling shoulder. "I am so sorry. Sneakers passed away on the operating table. His little body just couldn't handle the stress of the surgery."

Tara didn't hear anything the vet said after the words "Sneakers passed away." The shell-shocked girl fell to the floor and sobbed. "Sneakers! Oh, Sneakers! No, you can't be dead!" She pounded the floor in grief as Dr. Henning kneeled down and hugged her.

"It's okay to cry," he said. "Sneakers was a loyal and super pet. I know you're going to miss him very much because he's been a part of your life for a long time."

"I helped kill him," she bawled. "If I had listened to you, Sneakers would still be alive!"

"You made a decision that you thought was the right one at the time. No one can fault you for that."

"But I was wrong—and now Sneakers is dead."

* * *

For the next few days, Tara was an emotional wreck. She couldn't eat or sleep because of her grief and guilt. Her schoolwork suffered, and she was a drag around her classmates. She wouldn't smile, not even when her best friend Sandra came over to the house wearing a fright wig and funny false teeth.

"Girl, you better snap out of this funk," warned Sandra.

"With Sneakers gone, it's just eating away at my heart," Tara replied. "Why didn't I listen to the vet? Why did I have to be so selfish and think only of me and not Sneakers? Who knows how long he could have lived. All I know is he's dead—because of me."

Suddenly, Donnell's dog, Sampson, interrupted their conversation by letting out a frightened yelp. The kids ran into the hallway where Sampson was growling, barking, and backing up in fear. They looked around, but saw nothing.

"Donnell," said Tara, "what's wrong with Sampson?"

"I don't know," her brother replied. "He was lying in the hallway when all of a sudden he let out this yelp—you know, like when Sneakers would bop him on the nose. Now look at him. He's barking at nothing."

"He's scared of something," said Tara. "The hair on his back is sticking straight up."

"That's not like him. What's wrong, Sampson?" Donnell went over to calm down the dog. But Sampson, his eyes staring straight ahead, kept barking. Finally, Donnell grabbed the dog by the collar and ushered him outside.

THWACK!

"Hey, did you hear that, Sandra?" Tara asked.

"No, what?"

"It sounded like a bang. Almost like . . ." She began to cry again. "Almost like what Sneakers would do with his brush. He'd pick it up and bang it on the floor whenever he wanted to be fed or groomed."

THWACK!

"There it is again!" Tara jumped to her feet and ran into the bathroom, wishing she'd see Sneakers there, but knowing she wouldn't. She found his brush in the middle of the floor—the spot where Sneakers would drag it before dropping it—and not by the vent where she always left it.

As she picked up the brush, her heart felt so empty, so lonely—and so guilty. Tears started to flow again down Tara's cheeks.

"What's wrong?" asked Sandra, peeking in the doorway.

"I thought I heard Sneakers playing with his brush. He would be if it hadn't been for me."

"Will you stop beating yourself up over this? You need cheering up. Let's have some of your mama's oatmeal cookies." Sandra opened the refrigerator and poured each of them a glass of milk. She sat the glasses down on the kitchen table and opened the tin of cookies. "Now eat."

Tara halfheartedly took a bite and had a sip of milk. She put her glass down and said, "I wish I could get over these feelings of guilt."

"Hey, you're making a mess," said Sandra.

"What do you mean?"

"You're spilling milk."

"Huh?" Drops of milk dotted Tara's side of the table. "I don't know how I could have done it. I just had a little sip." Tara got a paper towel and was about to wipe up the milk when she looked closer at the splatters. "You know how Sneakers used to dip his paw in my glass? A couple of these drops almost look like paw prints."

Sandra rolled her eyes and groaned. "Do you think you could give it a rest? This is getting old."

Tara's mother entered the kitchen with an odd look on her face. "The weirdest thing just happened to me," she told them. "I was upstairs getting a big paper bag out of the closet to fill with old clothes for the Salvation Army. Well, I left it on the floor for a minute and I heard a rustling sound—you know, the kind that Sneakers made when he jumped into an empty bag. I turned around and—I know this sounds ridiculous—but I could have sworn I saw it move. I thought Sneakers was inside the bag. Now isn't that the silliest thing?"

* * *

Late that night, Tara's dad came home from a long day at the office, peeked into her room, and saw that she was reading in bed. "What are you still doing up?" he asked.

"I can't sleep."

"Sneakers?"

"Yes."

"We all miss him," Clarence admitted. "Even me. I know Sneakers and I had our differences—my, how he riled me up by playing with my ties—but he was a good cat. It's okay to grieve for him, but life goes on."

"Everyone tells me it's not my fault, but in my heart I know I helped kill him."

"Now stop that, honey. Sneakers didn't have long for this world, and he would have suffered had he lived. He had a quick and painless death—maybe it was all for the best that it happened this way."

"I wish I could believe that."

Her father gave her a big hug and kiss. "Try to get some sleep. I love you."

Clarence tiptoed into his bedroom because he didn't want to wake up Clarice. In the darkness, he tossed his clothes on the chair and draped his tie over the closet door handle before crawling into bed. He was just about to fall asleep when he heard a scratching sound on the closet door.

He sat up and listened carefully, but didn't hear anything again. *It sounded like Sneakers,* he thought. Then he shook his head. *Tara has been so hung up on that cat of hers. Now she's got me hearing things.*

* * *

About 1 A.M., Tara experienced the strangest sensation— that Sneakers had pounced onto her bed. She felt her blanket press down under soft, little steps until they stopped by her left hand.

I can almost feel Sneakers right here with me, putting his paw under my hand and laying his head on top of it, she told herself. *Is that a purr? Am I hearing a purr? Yes! I think I feel him holding my hand!* She started to reach over with her right hand to pet him, but stopped herself. *Tara, don't move. I like this feeling, and I don't want to ruin it. But what if there's nothing there. What if I'm just imagining this? No, it's real. It's Sneakers' spirit. It has to be him. He feels so good, so warm.* She lay perfectly still, savoring the feeling and remembering all the good times she had with her cat. Tara still felt sad and missed him terribly, but slowly the feelings of guilt that had consumed her heart and soul began to melt away. A smile soon crept across her lips.

* * *

The next morning, Clarence was getting dressed when he reached for his tie on the closet door handle. But it wasn't there. He looked around on the floor and finally found it—underneath his bed. *If I didn't know better,* he told himself, *I'd bet that Sneakers came back to pull off another one of his tie tricks. I wonder how it got there. Hey, wait a minute. That scratching sound last night. Could it be? Nah!*

Across the hall, Tara awoke to a little tug of a strand of her hair. She opened her eyes and expected to see Sneakers before reality quickly sunk in. But for the first time since her cat had died, Tara didn't wake up suffering from guilt pangs. In fact, she felt happy and relieved.

Tara bounded down the stairs and chirped a cheery "good morning" to her parents at the kitchen table.

"It's nice to see you in a good mood for a change," said Clarence.

"I feel happy," said Tara.

"That's my girl," Clarice beamed.

"You know," Clarence said with an embarrassed chuckle, "I must miss that darn cat more than I thought. I put my tie on the closet door handle when I went to bed, and as I was falling asleep I heard a scratching noise. This morning, I found my tie under the bed. How it got there, I don't know. And then I said out loud, 'Sneakers, have you come back to torment me?' "

Tara's parents laughed.

Tara nodded knowingly. "Daddy," she said, "don't laugh. Sneakers really *was* here."

"What are you talking about?" asked Clarice.

"His spirit came back," she stated flatly. "Yesterday, I

heard his brush drop, and I saw splatters of milk that only he could have made. Mama, you heard an empty paper bag move. And even Sampson barked at something no one could see. It had to be Sneakers' ghost.

"Last night, I felt him jump on my bed and hold my hand. I even heard him purr. Now I know why he returned. He knew that I loved him very much, and he understood that I tried to make the right decision about the operation. He came back to show me that he doesn't blame me for what happened to him and that I shouldn't feel guilty anymore. And you know what? I don't."

A yawning, sleepy-eyed Donnell trudged into the kitchen, scratching his head. "Guess how I woke up this morning?" he grumbled. "I heard all my things fall off the table by my bed. Now how do you suppose that happened?"

SPIKE'S REVENGE

Gavin Tinsley and his sister Amber could have treated their bulldog, Spike, so much better than they did. They weren't cruel to him or anything like that. They were simply irresponsible.

But Spike got even. Boy, did he get even.

* * *

When they got Spike as a puppy from the animal shelter, the kids, who were in grade school at the time, were thrilled. They played with Spike every day. They took turns walking and feeding him. They bathed him and taught him simple tricks like barking on command and shaking hands.

The bulldog was so ugly he was cute: short bowed legs, small bent ears, squinty brown eyes, squashed black nose, dirty off-white coat, and big droopy jowls.

By the time both kids were in junior high school, the novelty of having a dog had worn off. And it showed. Spike was always getting hurt or into trouble because Gavin and Amber were such careless owners.

One time, Spike was sitting on Gavin's lap in the back seat of the family car as it roared down the highway. Gavin lowered the window so Spike could stick out his nose. The dog then climbed on the door handle until more than half his body was hanging outside.

"Better get Spike back in, or he's liable to fall out," said Gavin's father.

"He's okay, Dad," said Gavin. "He's enjoying the breeze, sucking in the air."

Spike's ears perked up when he spotted a herd of cows. He let out a growl and then dove out of the speeding car. He rolled on the gravel shoulder of the road, stood up, wobbled, and then collapsed. The Tinsley's car screeched to a stop and Gavin leapt out.

"Spike! Spike!" The dog lifted his head, whimpered, and went limp. The Tinsleys rushed him to the animal clinic where he was treated for a concussion and a broken rib.

Gavin's parents made him pay for the veterinarian bills out of the money he earned mowing lawns.

Shortly after Spike recovered, Amber nearly killed him by her thoughtlessness. Rather than throw the chicken bones from dinner into the garbage, she dumped them in Spike's food bowl.

She should have known better. Chicken bones are bad for a dog because they splinter easily and can get lodged in its throat. That's what happened to Spike. As he gobbled up the chicken bones, he began gagging and whining in pain. Her father managed to dislodge the bone, but not before it had cut the inside of the dog's throat.

Six months later, Spike was sunning himself on the front steps of the house while Gavin talked with two buddies. When a classmate rode by on his bicycle, Gavin looked at the dog and, as a joke, shouted, "Sic him, Spike!" The dog charged across the lawn and, yelping all the way, ran out into the street to chase the bicycle. He never saw the car until the driver slammed on the brakes.

Spike took a glancing blow off the side of the front tire. Once again, he was rushed to the vet's and this time he was treated for a serious shoulder injury, cuts, and bruises. Gavin's lawn income shrank some more.

Two months later, Amber was home alone when she saw a mouse in the utility room. So she found a box of rat poison, opened it up, and put it down on the floor. Carelessly, she placed the poison, a white powder, right near Spike's food bowl which, as usual, was empty because she had forgotten to feed him.

Later that day, Amber found Spike whimpering, lying on his side on the kitchen floor. "What's wrong, Spike? Are you sick?" Then she noticed white powder caked around the edges of his mouth.

"Uh, oh," she said. "This looks like the rat poison I put down." Amber ran into the utility room and discovered that the box of rat poison was nearly empty.

So Spike made yet another trip to the vet's. This time, Amber's baby-sitting money went to pay the medical bills.

Spike became more of a chore than the Tinsley kids had planned. Because they had other interests in school, Spike wasn't receiving the attention from them that he deserved—and needed.

Rather than walk him like they were supposed to twice a day, they often let him out the door to wander around the neighborhood. More than once, an angry neighbor called to complain that Spike had left a mess in their front yard or had dug up a flower bed.

Spike loved to dig holes and roll around in the dirt and mud. As a result, he was often filthy. In fact, he stunk. Between his bad breath and body odor, you didn't have to see or hear him to know he was in the room. Despite his smelly presence, the kids seldom gave Spike a bath.

They began leaving him outside more and more. During the days, they would chain him out in the backyard while they attended school and their parents worked. But when the weather turned cold or rainy and they were gone all day, the Tinsleys kept him in the basement.

When their parents suggested finding a new home for Spike, Gavin and Amber howled in protest. "We can't get rid of Spike," said Gavin. "We've had him for six years. He's our dog. He's part of our family."

"But you don't take care of him," said their mother Lydia.

"We'll try to do a better job," Amber pledged. "We promise."

It was a shallow promise.

One Saturday, when both parents were working and Gavin was mowing lawns, Amber went over to her friend's house. She left Spike inside the house and didn't bother putting him in the basement, because she planned on returning home in an hour. However, after she arrived at her friend's, they decided to spend the day at the mall—and Amber totally forgot about Spike.

Stuck inside for the entire day with no food or water and no company or toys to play with, the bored bulldog began chewing on the leg of a wooden chair in the kitchen. After Spike had his fill of gnawed chair leg, he ambled into the living room where he spotted an electrical cord that snaked from a wall socket to a lamp. He started chomping on the cord.

That was a fatal mistake.

When the Tinsleys returned home late that afternoon, they were so busy that they failed to notice Spike hadn't greeted them. About a half hour after she arrived, Amber asked, "Has anyone seen Spike?"

Lydia looked out the back window. "He's not tied up. Did he slip free of his collar again?"

"No, Mom, I didn't chain him outside," Amber replied. "I left him in the house."

"Amber," her mother muttered disapprovingly. "You shouldn't have left him cooped up inside all day. He must be here someplace. Spike, where are you?"

After a quick search, they found Spike dead behind the couch. "He must have been chewing on the cord when he got electrocuted," Ed explained.

"Poor Spike," said Gavin.

A tearful Amber murmured, "I feel so bad."

* * *

The next night, Amber was awakened from a sound sleep by an eerie growl—a low, rumbling "grrrrr." *Spike?* she thought. *No, silly, it can't be him—he's dead.* Still half asleep,

Amber stumbled to the window, opened it, and looked out in her backyard. *Nothing out there.* Moments later, she made a scary discovery. *Hey, the growling isn't coming from outside. It's coming from in this room!*

The "grrrr" sent shivers down her spine. It sounded like the angry, threatening growl of an animal ready to pounce on its prey.

Not knowing what she'd find, Amber fearfully peeked under her bed, behind the dresser, and in her closet. The search revealed nothing—except the mysterious growl was following her wherever she went in her room.

Amber dashed out into the hallway where she stopped and listened. Silence. *Should I wake up Mom and Dad? Nah, they'll just say I was dreaming. Maybe I was.*

She returned to her room, climbed into bed, took a deep breath to relax, closed her eyes, and . . .

"Grrrrrrr."

The frightened teen rolled over on her stomach, threw the pillow over her head, and held it tightly against her ears until the growl faded away.

When she woke up at daybreak, Amber lay frozen in bed, wondering if she would hear the spooky growl again. The only sounds reaching her ears were the birds chirping outside her window and the thumping bass of Gavin's stereo.

I must have imagined that growl, she told herself. *It's probably my conscience doing a number on me. If only I had put Spike outside, he wouldn't be dead now.* She figured that the strange growl wasn't worth mentioning to anyone.

The following night Gavin woke up, choking, coughing, and retching from a putrid stench. Every time he took a breath, he felt like gagging. He covered his mouth with his hand, bolted for the window, opened it, and gulped several deep breaths of fresh air.

When he walked back toward his bed, the odor grew stronger. *Man, where is this smell coming from?* he wondered. He flicked on the light and looked around the room, but couldn't find the source of the stench. *It stinks like a combination of Spike's bad breath and his body odor after getting all hot and sweaty—only much stronger. Yuck.* After checking every square inch of his room, he was dumbfounded. *This is so weird. The odor seems to be coming from my bed and nowhere else in my room. It can't be me, can it? I shower every day.*

He turned on the fan, opened his window and door, and soon cleared the room of the smell. Gavin decided not to say anything about the stench because he was afraid the rest of the family would laugh and blame it on him.

That morning, Amber walked barefoot into the kitchen and asked, "Mom, have you seen a brown loafer? I can only find my left one."

"Is it from the pair we bought you last week?" her mother, Lydia, asked.

"Yes. I've looked everywhere for it."

"Amber, you better find it," her mother said sternly. "Now if you had just picked up your shoes and put them away, this wouldn't have happened."

"But, Mom . . ."

Just then Gavin entered the kitchen. "Hey, does anyone know where my copy of *The Red Badge of Courage* is?" he asked. "I had it in my room last night and now it's not there.

It's a paperback and I need it for English class."

"What is it with you kids?" muttered Lydia, shaking her head. "You lose shoes and books. Take some responsibility, please. Goodness knows you didn't show any when it came to poor Spike."

The next night, Amber decided to sleep with her bedroom door open, hoping she would never hear that scary growling again. She didn't. Instead, as Amber was dozing off, she was jolted by a different noise.

What's that? she asked herself. *Someone scraping their fingernails across my desk? No, it's more like gnawing. What if it's a rat?* She shuddered. *Don't you dare put your feet down on the floor.* The gnawing continued for another few minutes until Amber couldn't stand it any longer.

"Mom! Dad!" she yelled. "Come here, quick!"

Her parents and brother rushed into her room. Ed flicked on the light and worriedly asked, "What's the matter, Amber?"

"I heard an animal gnawing in my room. I think it's a rat."

They searched the room, checking the baseboards and looking behind the furniture. "Amber, I don't know what you may have heard, but there's no sign of any rat or other critter around here," said Ed.

"I know what I heard, and it definitely was chewing. And I wasn't dreaming it either," she declared.

After her family left the room, it took Amber a long time to fall asleep. The next morning, she was about to put the gnawing incident behind her, but she couldn't—not after what happened when she went to get a sweater out of a lower drawer of her dresser. She grabbed the wooden drawer knobs, felt something odd, looked down, and screamed. The left knob had been chewed up.

The gnawing sound! Some animal was in my room last night!

Her parents immediately called the exterminator, hoping to find the animal and get rid of it.

Late that night, Gavin was reading in bed when he heard an unexpected noise. He put his book down and sat up, trying to identify it.

Rip . . . grunt, grunt . . . rip.

What in the world could that be? Gavin wondered. The moment he hopped out of bed, the noise stopped. He looked around his room. Everything seemed fine, so he went back to bed. He picked up his book and began reading again. Suddenly, the noise returned.

Rip . . . grunt, grunt . . . rip.

I'm getting tired of all this. Last time it was a terrible smell. And now strange noises. But just as quickly as the bizarre rips and grunts started, they stopped.

Early the next morning, when it was still dark, Gavin got up to go to the bathroom. Yawning and stretching, he reached the doorway of his room when he tripped and sprawled into the hallway with a loud thud.

The fall knocked the wind out of him. *Ow, that hurt. What did I trip over?* He staggered to his feet and turned on the light to his room. The bedroom carpeting by the doorway had been torn loose from its tacking and was curled up about six inches (15 cm). *How could the carpeting have been pulled up like this?* And then it dawned on him. *The ripping*

and grunting noise from last night! What is going on?
* * *

"There has to be a logical explanation," said Ed as the family sat around the breakfast table. "The exterminator is coming today, and he'll capture the animal that gnawed on Amber's dresser drawer and ripped Gavin's carpeting. Then we'll get to the bottom of this problem."

"It would be easy to solve if Spike were around," said Amber. "We would have blamed it on him, because they're all things he was capable of doing."

"You know, you've got a point there," Gavin noted. "There's something I haven't told you. The night before last, I gagged on this awful stench that smelled like Spike at his worst. And, no, it wasn't me, Amber."

"Now that you mention it," she said, "I heard a spooky growling noise in my room, and it scared me half to death."

"Maybe it's Spike, and he's come back to haunt us," said Gavin with a big grin.

Everyone laughed. But no one took him seriously—yet.
* * *

The exterminator found no evidence that any rodent or other animal had invaded the house. But the news didn't ease the concern of the kids, because now there was no simple way to explain the events of the past few nights.

When Amber and Gavin went to their bedrooms, they wondered what new, disturbing surprise awaited them. Their worrying kept them up half the night, although they didn't see or hear anything strange. They were both so tired that when they finally did get to sleep, they slept very hard.

The next morning, Gavin stumbled into the kitchen.

113

"Good morning, Mr. Smooth," joked his mother.

Gavin looked down at his pants. "I tripped over my cuff," he explained. "I didn't notice that it's still torn. Mom, I thought you had sewed it up last week after Spike ripped it when he got mad at me for teasing him."

"I did mend it a week ago," Lydia said. "Let me see your pants cuff." After examining it, she pursed her lips. "Hmmm, this is odd. It's a new tear. When did you last wear these pants?"

"Not since you fixed them. They've been hanging in the closet until now."

"If I didn't know better, I'd say this tear was Spike's handiwork," she said. "But it couldn't be, because I mended your pants the day after he died."

"Mom, remember that crack I made about Spike haunting us? What if . . ."

Amber burst into the kitchen, holding several sheets of crumpled up, tattered paper in her fist. "Look what I found in my backpack!" she cried. "My social studies report. It's all torn up and it's due today!"

Gavin looked at the tattered pages and said, "There are puncture marks made from teeth all over the pages. An animal did this."

"You mean the mysterious animal that has been harassing us that no one can find?" asked Amber.

"That—or a dog."

"What do you mean, Gavin?"

"Don't you see what's going on here?" Gavin said. "Spike has been *haunting* us! After his death, you heard him growl, and I smelled him. Then he chewed on your dresser drawer and yanked up my carpeting. This morning, I found my pants ripped, and you found your report torn."

"Oh, great," huffed Amber. "What am I going to tell my teacher? That my dog ate my homework? I don't have a dog, because he's dead. But I do have a brother who is certifiably wacko."

"I'm telling you, Spike is haunting us!" Gavin insisted.

"But why?"

"I don't know. Maybe he's trying to get even. Let's face it, we weren't exactly the best owners."

"We weren't ever mean to him," Amber countered.

"No, but everything bad that ever happened to him—the injuries, the poisoning, the electrocution—was because of us. It was always our fault."

Amber sat down, reflected on what her brother said and nodded. "We should have spent more time with him, cared for him better, and shown him how much we loved him. I admit, I wasn't very responsible. Maybe his ghost is trying to teach us a lesson."

"Mom, what do you think?" asked Gavin.

"I'm willing to keep an open mind, although I believe the events over the last week have been caused by a real animal that's loose in our house," Lydia answered. "There's really no proof that Spike's ghost even exists. Now then, since you both brought up the subject of responsibility, how about helping me weed the flower beds tomorrow?"

Both kids groaned.

* * *

"Hey, what's this?" asked Gavin after his trowel struck an object in the flower bed. He dug a little deeper and, to his astonishment, pulled out a paperback book. "Well, will you look at this! It's my missing *Red Badge of Courage!*" He pushed more dirt aside. "There's something else in here." He plucked a shoe from the hole.

"That's my missing loafer!" shouted Amber. "What's that doing in there?"

After taking a closer look at the two items, Gavin announced, "There are teeth marks on them. It had to be from Spike's ghost."

"It *could* be his ghost," corrected Lydia. "It's also possible that Spike swiped the book and shoe from your rooms and buried them out here before his death."

"What was the date he died?" Gavin asked.

"It happened on your Uncle Frank's birthday," replied his mother. "It was the 21st."

Gavin held up a dirty envelope that had been in the book. "This envelope had an invitation in it to the sports banquet," he said. "I used it as a bookmark. It's postmarked the 22nd."

"That means Spike buried these things *after* his death!" Amber declared. "Is that proof enough, Mom?"

Lydia stood up, brushed the dirt off her pants, and admitted, "I'm stunned. Maybe Spike's ghost *has* been haunting you two after all."

"How do we make him stop?" asked Gavin.

"It's obvious that he's very angry at both of you for neglecting him—and for good reason. Maybe there's some way you can make it up to him."

"How?" asked Amber. "By being more responsible? He's dead—we can't help him anymore."

"I'm sure you two will think of something."

* * *

Amber and Gavin knew their mother was right. They had to become more responsible—and stick to their responsibilities. Soon after their conversation with their mother, Amber began caring for an elderly neighbor's basset hound and Gavin began volunteering at the animal shelter. And Spike's ghost never tormented the kids again.

RESCUE FROM THE BEYOND

Hamlet, a gentle giant of a Great Dane, loved his mistress Megan O'Connor so much that nothing could keep him from protecting her—not even death.

The huge Great Dane stood tall and proud, measuring 30 inches (76 cm) from the ground to his shoulders and weighing 120 pounds (54 kg), a full 40 pounds (18 kg) more than his 13-year-old mistress. His shiny, short-haired coat matched the tan color of a fawn's hide and featured streaks of dark brown from his spine to his belly. Setting him apart from other Great Danes, he sported a dark brown ear and a light tan one. Despite his size, Hamlet put most people at ease because his large brown eyes twinkled with the friendliness of a puppy.

Hamlet had been Megan's faithful companion ever since he was a pup and she was three years old. Her parents bought the dog for protection because they didn't live in the best of neighborhoods.

It didn't take long before Hamlet towered over the little girl. But even as he outgrew her, he remained as gentle and lovable as a lamb. During her preschool years, Megan could do most anything to him—playfully yank on his tail, squeeze him around the neck—and Hamlet would take it all in stride, never growling or snapping at her.

The freckle-faced, red-haired wisp of a girl loved to hop on his back, hold onto his neck, and ride him around the backyard like a pony. Hamlet enjoyed the attention and would trot proudly. Other times, with a rope tied to his collar, he would pull her while she sat in her little red wagon. But despite her pleas for him to go faster, Hamlet knew better. He would never do anything to hurt her.

Despite his sweet disposition, Hamlet was fiercely loyal and protective of Megan. Whenever her parents scolded her, Hamlet would sit in front of her and whine, as though he were trying to block the angry words from reaching Megan. He wouldn't dare growl at her parents, whom he loved as well, but he would let them know that he was upset.

Outside, if Megan started playfully wrestling with one of the neighborhood kids, Hamlet would scamper around them and bark. If he didn't hear her say "It's okay, Hamlet," he would gingerly grab her opponent by the shirt or pants with his teeth and drag the kid away from Megan.

Hamlet acted as Megan's canine guardian angel and instinctively sensed danger. One time, when Megan was eight, she was taking him for a walk when a stranger drove up and asked for directions. Hamlet barked and snarled at the man, and Megan had a difficult time holding onto the dog's leash.

"Hamlet! Stop it!" she ordered. "I'm sorry, Mister. He usually isn't like this."

She gave the man directions and he drove off. A few days later, Megan saw the man's face on the news. He had been arrested for the attempted kidnapping of a six-year-old girl only a few blocks away—on the same day Megan had encountered him.

Hamlet saved her again during a visit to her grandparents' farm when she was ten.

Megan had wandered over to a fenced-off area to check on two newborn calves. Wanting to get a better look, she climbed over the fence and began petting them. Megan didn't realize that her innocent actions were viewed by the mother cow as threatening to the newborns.

With Megan not paying any attention to the cow behind her, the animal lowered its head, charged, and rammed into her. Megan went sprawling face-first into the muck. The angry cow then used its nose to roll Megan over and was getting ready to step on her.

Seeing his mistress attacked, Hamlet sprang into action. He leaped over the fence and bit into the cow's jaw and held on until Megan could crawl away. Once the dog knew that Megan was safe, he let go of the cow and continued to bark at it. Then he jumped over the fence and ran to Megan, who was bruised and dirty but otherwise unhurt.

Those weren't the only times Hamlet acted as a hero.

Twice when Megan and her parents had gone out for the evening, burglars had attempted to break into their house by busting a window and climbing inside. And twice they fled when Hamlet confronted them.

But more than a protector, Hamlet was Megan's loyal companion.

The dog would sit on his hind legs and look Megan in the eye to sense her mood. If she felt sad, Hamlet would bury his head under her arm or lick her hand. If she felt upbeat, he would bring her a ball in the hopes of playing with her outside. Sometimes he tried to get her to dance by resting his big paws on her shoulders and slurping her face. But when he did, he always managed to keep most of his weight on his hind legs so that he wouldn't accidentally push her down.

During the day, when Megan was at school, Hamlet spent most of his time outside in the fenced-in backyard. He liked to play with one of her old teddy bears, tossing and shaking it. The O'Connors figured he liked the teddy bear because it carried Megan's scent. But he played so rough that he had already chewed up three of the bears and was on his fourth by the time Megan turned 12.

He never played with the teddy bear when Megan was home because he'd rather be with her. Often when she watched television, Megan would lie on the floor with Hamlet and use his back as a pillow. Whenever she talked on the phone—which was a lot—Hamlet would spread out on the floor by her side. She would stroke his ears until he felt so relaxed that he would fall asleep.

At night, just before Megan hopped into bed, the two carried out a ritual. Hamlet would lie on his back and Megan would rub his tummy. Then she'd give him a big kiss.

"Hamlet, you're my best friend," Megan would tell him. "I can't imagine living without you. Promise you'll never leave me." He'd nudge her hand and bark as if he were giving her his word.

But then the unthinkable happened. Megan was stroking his tummy one day when she noticed a lump on his right side below his rib cage. The lump grew larger and he began losing his appetite and energy. Alarmed, the O'Connors took him to the veterinarian, who performed several tests on the dog. The diagnosis sent Megan into a tailspin of grief.

"I'll give it to you straight," the vet told Megan and her parents. "Hamlet is suffering from a deadly form of cancer, and it has spread throughout his body. There is no hope of recovery."

"Please, doctor, there must be something you can do," Megan pleaded with trembling lips.

"Megan, the only humane thing to do is to put him to sleep soon so he doesn't have to suffer. He's in pain."

Megan was devastated, walking around in a daze, not wanting to believe that she would soon have to tell her best friend good-bye forever. The night before the dreaded moment, Megan scratched Hamlet's tummy for the last time, unable to look at the large deadly lump that was responsible for her terrible sadness.

"Hamlet, I'll miss you so much, so very much. Promise you'll come back from dog heaven and see me, okay?" Hamlet, wincing in pain, gave a soft bark.

The next morning, Megan led Hamlet into the kitchen. "I'm going to the vet's with you, Dad," she said. "I should be with Hamlet. I want the last thing he feels to be my arms holding him. I don't want him to die with strangers."

"Megan, are you sure you want to put yourself through all this?" he asked.

"I'm sure. Hamlet has always been there for me. He's protected me, he's been by my side when I needed someone to talk to, he's kept me warm, and he's given me so much love. I've got to be there for him."

At the vet's, Megan and her father took Hamlet into the examining room. The dog lay down on the floor and put his head in Megan's lap. Megan stroked his ears and, through her tear-filled eyes, she whispered, "I don't want you to go, but I know it's for the best. You'll always be a part of me, Hamlet. You'll always be there in my heart. I love you."

He looked up at her with those big brown eyes as though he understood he was about to die. Megan leaned down and kissed him. She cradled his head in her arms as the doctor injected her beloved dog with a solution designed to kill painlessly and instantly. Hamlet then closed his eyes for the last time. And Megan cried.

* * *

Megan and her father wrapped Hamlet in a sheet, put him in the back of their van, and drove home in near silence. They went out to the backyard and dug his grave, making sure it was neat with smooth sides. Mr. O'Connor then laid Hamlet down in the hole. For a dog that was so large in life, so big-hearted, he seemed so small to Megan. She placed his stuffed teddy bear next to his body and covered him over with dirt. After filling the grave, Megan kneeled down and said, "At least you'll always be near me, Hamlet."

For weeks, Megan's heart ached. She missed her dog so much. "I'll wake up in the morning and think he's at the foot of my bed like he always was, but he's not there," she told her mother. "When I talk on the phone, I automatically try to pet him, but he's not there. I miss rubbing his tummy at night."

"I know how difficult it is to lose Hamlet," said her mother. "But time has a way of healing your sorrow."

"It's strange, Mom, but there are times when I almost can feel him next to me. Like when I'm reading in bed, I'll think he's resting near my feet, keeping them warm."

"When you feel up to it," said her mother, "let's get another dog, a puppy that you can raise and train and —"

"Get another dog?" gasped Megan, shocked by the suggestion. "I couldn't. I just couldn't. No dog could ever replace Hamlet. He's still my dog. Even if he's not here physically anymore, he's here in my heart. Another dog? No way!"

One night, about three months after Hamlet's death, Megan was home alone, watching television. Shortly after midnight, her parents called, telling Megan they were having such a good time at their high school reunion that they would be home very late. They reminded her again to make sure the doors and windows were locked and to leave the outdoor lights on.

Megan wasn't afraid to be alone, but she didn't feel quite the confidence she used to have when Hamlet was alive. With her Great Dane by her side, she felt perfectly safe, knowing that he would protect her. She felt much more vulnerable now, but not scared.

About 1 A.M., she turned off the TV, checked all the doors and windows, and went to bed. The moment her head hit the pillow, she began dreaming about Hamlet. He was romping around in the backyard, happily tossing and shaking his teddy bear. But suddenly he stopped playing. He stood still with his ears and tail perked up. Then he growled and bared his teeth before pacing back and forth, frantically barking louder and louder.

He barked so loudly in her dream that Megan woke up. For one fleeting moment, she expected to find Hamlet at the foot of her bed. But then she became clear-headed enough to realize it was all a dream.

Suddenly, she heard a thump coming from the family room and the sound of the sliding glass door opening.

"Mom? Dad?" she called out. "Is that you?"

The sleepy-eyed girl walked out into the hallway, wondering why her parents hadn't used the side door that led to the attached garage.

"Is somebody there?" She flicked on the family room light—and froze in terror. There, not more than ten feet (3 m) away from Megan, stood a burly man in a black T-shirt, black pants, and a black baseball cap pulled down to his eyebrows.

"Don't move!" he ordered, whipping out from his waist a snub-nosed revolver.

"Oh, please, don't shoot me!" Megan stammered.

"Then do as I tell you," he snapped. "Are you alone?"

Megan nodded.

"I need money and jewelry," he said. "Show me where those things are, and you won't get hurt."

Fear left Megan's mouth bone dry and her legs feeling like jelly as he marched her down the hallway to her parents' bedroom. *Oh, Hamlet, I wish you were here,* she thought. *You'd protect me. You'd save me.*

She opened up a drawer and pointed to the jewelry box inside. The intruder rummaged around and pulled out a couple of gold necklaces and rings. "That's all? Where's the rest?"

"There isn't any more. We're not rich or—"

"You're lying!" His eyes erupted in a blaze of fury, and he lunged for Megan. She screamed with fright and bolted into the family room where he grabbed her from behind and threw her hard to the floor.

He stood over her for what seemed like an eternity but was only a matter of seconds. *Is he going to hurt me?* she wondered. *Is he going to kill me? Oh how I wish Hamlet was still alive.*

Suddenly, the intruder lurched backward as though some invisible force had shoved him. "Hey, what's going on?" he shouted. He was pushed back again, this time against a chair where he lost his balance and flipped over on his back. The fall knocked the gun out of his hand.

Megan leaped to her feet and couldn't believe her eyes. The intruder was rolling around the floor, his hands wildly trying to fend off an unseen force. "Leave me alone!" he cried out. "Get off of me! *Ahhhhh!*"

At first, Megan thought he was suffering from a seizure or hallucination from drugs. But then, to her astonishment, she saw the skin on both of his cheeks split open and blood trickle down his face. Bloody scratches crisscrossed his hands as he desperately fought the invisible force.

Megan didn't know what was happening to him, and she

wasn't about to stay around a moment longer to find out. She grabbed the gun and fled the house. She raced over to the next-door neighbors and pounded on their door.

"There's a burglar in my house!" she yelled. "Call 911!"

The police responded within minutes and surrounded her home. Then they carefully made their way inside and found the intruder, bleeding and dazed, as he staggered to his feet. "I give up," he said. "Just keep that big dog away from me."

The police threw handcuffs on the burglar and hustled him out the front door while Megan stayed next door with the neighbors. "I don't understand," he muttered to the cops. "The dog was invisible when he attacked me and then all of a sudden, while he's mauling me, I could see him. Am I nuts?"

"The only thing you are is in deep trouble," said an officer, shoving him into the patrol car.

Megan, still shuddering from her ordeal, eventually walked back into her house where investigators were examining the crime scene. "Are you all right?" asked the detective in charge.

Megan nodded. "I'm okay, but I just can't stop shaking. How did he get in?"

"The intruder had a tool that pried the sliding glass door off its track. Then he opened it and slipped inside. Thank goodness your dog came to the rescue."

Megan felt stunned. "Dog? What dog?" she asked.

"The one that attacked the burglar. The one that bit him and clawed him up. I think he said it was a Great Dane. You do have one, don't you?"

"I had one but . . ." She never finished her sentence. Out of the corner of her eye, she spotted something through the sliding glass door that caused her heart to skip a beat. Under the outdoor lights, a Great Dane romped in the backyard. Tan, with stripes on his side, and one ear darker than the other.

"Hamlet!" Megan shrieked in joy. "Oh, Hamlet, you've come back!" She dashed out into the yard, aching to throw her arms around him. But before she could reach him, the dog vanished into the darkness by his grave where the beams of the lights fell short. Desperately, she searched the yard, but could find no trace of Hamlet.

Emotionally crushed, Megan sprawled over Hamlet's grave and cried until she could cry no more. But then, as she tried to catch her breath, she sensed a familiar presence by her side. And for a precious, lingering moment, she felt reunited with Hamlet. "You're here with me, aren't you?" she murmured. "You'll always be here with me—in spirit."